GOING
APE

GOING APE

How to Stop Talking About Your Relationship and Start Enjoying It

DR. JULIUS ROSEN

A Blue Cliff Editions Book
Edited by Arlene Harris Shulman

CB

CONTEMPORARY
BOOKS
CHICAGO · NEW YORK

Library of Congress Cataloging-in-Publication Data

Rosen, Julius.
    Going ape : how to stop talking about your relationship and start
enjoying it / Julius Rosen ; edited by Arlene Harris Shulman.
        p.   cm.
    "A Blue Cliff editions book."
    ISBN 0-8092-4507-8
    1. Communication in marriage.   2. Marital psychotherapy—
United States.   3. Interpersonal communication—United States.
I. Shulman, Arlene Harris.   II. Title.
HQ734.R756   1988
646.7'8—dc19   88-25726
                                                                         CIP

Published by Contemporary Books, Inc.
180 North Michigan Avenue, Chicago, Illinois 60601
Manufactured in the United States of America
Library of Congress Catalog Card Number: 88-25726
International Standard Book Number: 0-8092-4507-8

Published simultaneously in Canada by Beaverbooks, Ltd.
195 Allstate Parkway, Valleywood Business Park
Markham, Ontario L3R 4T8 Canada

This book is dedicated to my three loves:
Rose, my mama, the best in the world
Andrea, my daughter, my pride and joy
Yetta, my wife, my best friend and my special partner

Contents

Foreword

In an age when we can split atoms and have telephone conversations with friends who are thousands of miles away, it is incredible that we have not made any significant gains in solving the most crucial problem of all: how to get along with each other. Sadly, that old song "You Always Hurt the One You Love," seems truer now than ever. Conflict between countries is nothing compared to some of the marriages I've seen. What we need is a penicillin for relationships, something that will heal them quickly and give us a chance to get back on track.

Well, Dr. Julius Rosen has given us just such a magic bullet. Like penicillin, it alone isn't the answer—you still have to make other efforts to stay healthy. But the power he puts in your hand with this book is amazing in its capacity to mend a troubled relationship and put you on the road to closeness.

Everyone talks about being close, but talk is difficult to translate into actions. In *Going Ape*, Dr. Rosen gives all of us—patients and therapists alike—the courage to reach for intimacy, because he approaches it in a humorous, sensitive, even revolutionary way. There is a unique and wondrous beauty in achieving a fulfilling relationship so simply.

Dr. Rosen's ideas are on the leading edge of experiential therapy, particularly couples' therapy. He has taken Western psychological theory and integrated it with Eastern spiritual philosophy and practice, the combination of which yields a program that is neither Eastern nor Western, but humanistic. Just as Dr. Milton Erickson's unusual techniques freed a generation of therapists to encourage families to interact in a healthy way, Rosen frees the next generation of families and therapists by facilitating a genuine warmth within the family structure, starting with the core familial relationship: the couple.

I have had many discussions with Dr. Rosen about his technique, and I have tried some of his tactics. I'm delighted to report that his ideas work. If your relationship is in trouble, especially if you have managed to stay aloof from your partner, Rosen will manipulate you into getting close and actually enjoying yourselves. He does this in both subtle and obvious ways. Don't try to outguess him; just stay with the program.

As a therapist, I, as well as my patients, have fun with these methods. Far too many partners feel that pain and chaos are the burdens of relationships. This book will lift those burdens—and your spirits.

Milton Pereira, M.D.
New York, N.Y.
June 1988

Acknowledgments

Thanks to: Jason Shulman, for always believing in this book; Jackie Ogburn and Melinda Corey of Blue Cliff Editions for editorial assistance; Stacy Prince, for her brilliant editing; Dr. Milton Pereira, for encouraging me to share my ideas; and Arlene Harris Shulman, for finding a form in which my ideas could be effectively expressed.

Introduction

Action is eloquence.

William Shakespeare

Most people believe that the more they think and the more intellectual knowledge they acquire, the better prepared they are for being part of a couple. In reality, we have become so cerebral in our relating that we no longer see, feel, or touch each other. Our intellectual clutter keeps us from relating at all. This complex cognitive garbage serves to mask our fears and feelings. It hides our basic need for love, affection, caring, and tenderness. When we operate from this level, our partner reacts to the mask instead of the needs underneath. He or she answers our needs with more intellectualization, and thus our real needs are not met. Nobody gets fed, and both partners are left hungry. At this point, often the easiest road to take in a partnership is the wrong one: to treat it like an old coat—discard it and then move on.

Rational thinking does have a place in a couple's relationship, but it should not be a substitute for intimacy. For the very same rational thinking and intellectualization, so useful in other parts of our lives, will often hide feelings that are difficult to express, causing confusion in our personal lives. We do not like to expose such feelings as "Please take care of me," "I beg you to be with me," and "Don't let me be

1

alone." We mask them with accusations and complaints, saying, "You never talk to me" or "Why don't you hang your clothes up?"—and in reply we usually get intellectual statements such as "You're overreacting" or "Stop harping on me." When you answer a hidden fear with an intellectual statement, your partner will probably feel even more alone or abandoned, and this continues the vicious cycle of masked communication. Thus "rational" thinking becomes a weapon for most couples. It is only after you have achieved intimacy that you can hope to use such thinking to enhance your relationship.

This is a book that teaches couples not to think. It will teach you to step backward in human evolution, to learn a few lessons in primitive relating from our ancestors, the apes. It will take you to a time when communication was simple and direct and help you use the lessons you learn to make your communication clear and vital. *Going Ape* presents a method of getting back to basics by learning the art of Primitive Communication. Through Primitive Communication we remove our disguises and address our real needs. By uncluttering our minds of too much information about ourselves and others, we open the door to real and direct relating. We stand exposed, in our most primitive state, where our needs and those of our partner can be massaged verbally and physically.

When people see each other as soft and mutually dependent, they like each other. When they see each other as automatons, enemies, or competitors, they feel alienated and alone. This can lead people to strike out at themselves (usually through some form of substance abuse) or to abuse their partners, thus creating a power struggle in which they compete to abuse each other or change each other.

Primitive Communication helps couples show their vulnerability to each other by acting silly, being playful, and generally having a good time. This can include everything from placing obscene calls (to your partner, of course—what kind of a nut do you think I am?) to becoming a Cro-Magnon couple that relates simply through grunts and groans. Once the "sophisticated" words are extinguished, the defensive signals that couples are used to begin to fade.

At first, this may sound totally ridiculous. Two people who ordinarily relate in a sophisticated, cognitive fashion suddenly find themselves reduced to apes and are the better for it. It sounds hilarious. But humor is an essential ingredient in Primitive Communication. It is a crucial way to undercut the extreme intensity that smart people sometimes develop when they are in trouble. When there is too much intensity, couples can't talk to each other simply. No matter what one partner says to the other, things heat up. Both people react to such intensity, and their emotions build to a critical point. Humor helps to defuse the time bomb. It makes things simple again.

A successful primitive relationship is one in which people are free to learn about themselves and each other in a healthy way. It is one in which people do not misuse or blame each other. Each partner can reach out to the other to reveal the kind of human being he or she is and the kind of relationship he or she needs. The two actually begin to transmit healthy, clear messages to each other.

Let me say at this point that I feel a little frustrated by not being able to meet you. We are meeting as writer and reader, but we are not actually facing each other as two people trying to learn more about life and relationships. I wish we could shake hands now, because I would say, "Trust me." I want your relationship to get better; this is very important to me. I let all couples who work with me know how I feel about this right away, and since you are now working with me, it's something I want you to know.

It is important that you trust me, because I will be asking you in this book to do some pretty wacky things. I'm sure no one has ever asked you to "go ape" with your partner, especially without telling you why, but for now I ask you not to seek explanations—I want you to say bye-bye to "Why?" I know that your urge for an explanation may tempt you not to try new ways of expressing yourself, but put these urges aside. I'll help you fight these urges by encouraging you to be silly and absurd all the way. You will learn a new method of reaching your partner in nonjudgmental ways.

I do not claim Primitive Communication will eradicate all the problems between you and your partner. I do claim, however, that if you practice Primitive Communication, your problems will not eradicate your relationship. Primitive Communication offers a way for couples to learn to trust each other, to learn to make each other feel safe. Only in this kind of atmosphere can disagreements be worked out rather than cause a "walkout."

The wonderful thing about Primitive Communication is that it works quickly. It can begin to work in minutes. Most important, going ape is a lot of fun. It's playful, it's direct, and it works.

3

The Need for a Special Partner

I value relationships. A relationship is precious, too precious to throw out—yet I continually see people changing partners in search of "that special person." Before we do any changing, however, we need to know that we did our best with the partner we have. Most of the time all that's needed is a little fresh air, a little humor, and a few intimacy skills. When you develop intimacy skills, you learn how to protect your partner and your relationship.

Protection is an important part of having a special partner. You feel protected, and you protect the person you love. You are not alone. Even if you are separated physically because of work or travel, the feeling of protection stays with you. When apart, you store ideas, images, and feelings to share with your partner. Each event or emotion becomes part of both of you.

This protection is a kind of commitment that makes everything special. It is expressed in the phrase "in sickness and in health, 'til death do us part." Physically, if one has a disability, the other will make up for this deficit. If you cannot feed yourself, then your partner will feed you. If you cannot read, then your partner will read to you. If you cannot hear, then your partner will signal to you. Your partner becomes that missing part. You are spiritually intertwined. You can lean on each other. When you bond with your partner in this way, you will want to touch, feel, sense, share, laugh, cry, hold, reach, nurture, feed, stroke, and be with your partner—this is what life is really all about.

The special partner we choose becomes a best friend who makes life easier to bear and less lonely. He or she can make each day, month, and year of our lives a meaningful experience. Life can be frightening without this special person.

If your suffering from lack of intimacy with your partner has been acute, no doubt it has crossed your mind that perhaps you don't deserve that special relationship. I can tell you emphatically that you do deserve it. *You* are special, and you deserve a special partner.

This book will help you develop that bond, that special partnership. It will help you discover just how special your relationship is, and rather than throwing it away, you will treasure it for the rest of your life.

How to Use *Going Ape*

Going Ape consists of a warm-up section and seven basic topics that cover areas of concern for most couples. Each topic is divided into ideas, tactics and comments, and a task menu. The ideas give you some new ways of thinking; the tactics and comments teach you new ways to act. The task menu at the end of each topic encourages you once more to actually try doing some of the things I suggest.

You can either follow the organization I have laid out or peruse the Contents and go directly to a topic or tactic that interests you. A lot depends upon your situation in life. If you are in the midst of a major battle in your relationship, for example, you may want to start with Topic 1: "Problems, Problems, Problems." But whatever your situation, don't go straight to any topic before you read the "Seven-Day Warm-Up."

The "Seven-Day Warm-Up" will help downgrade your intellect in a very short time and serve as the basis for everything that follows. This warm-up introduces you to the four basic principles of Primitive Communication; in it you will learn to stop asking questions, to act like an ape (with all of the accompanying grunts and groans) and substitute the word *me* for I whenever speaking to your partner, to use words or

7

sounds when touching your partner, and to take advantage of the healthful effects of absurdity and humor. Because you will be learning a strange and exotic language that includes such phrases as "Me give you yummies" and "Me give huggy-poo," I have included a Primate Foreign Phrase Dictionary, which, along with the warm-up, will prepare you for the zany world of Primitive Communication.

Toward the end of the book, I will give you some theory and answer some questions you might have about Primitive Communication. But I hope after going through the book you will not feel a need to read that section. The most important thing you will need to use this book successfully is a willingness to put your rational mind aside and act instead of think. I'll be giving you a lot of help along the way.

By the way, if you are in a household with children, you'll want to keep your Primitive Communication between you and your partner. I do not want your kid to be asked at school, "What is two plus two?" only to reply, "Me know it's four." I also do not want Junior to say to the teacher, "Teach, me give huggy-poo." If this happens, Junior will be sent to the school nurse.

So for now, keep the secrets of this book between you and your partner. I encourage you and your partner to go ape, but for the time being we'll encourage Junior to walk the path to intellectual enlightenment.

The most important thing for you to remember as you read this book is that you can't be too absurd or too silly. Do not try to wipe that smile off your face as you do some of the zany things I ask you to do. The key is to surrender to zaniness.

Getting Started by Yourself

As you begin to share the ideas in this book, be careful how you include your partner. You may become excited about an idea. You feel that it will work, but that doesn't mean your partner will share your feelings. If your partner wants to engage in many of the activities, great; if not, then you have to take the responsibility to do things for yourself. You can make offers in a gentle way, but your partner has the right to refuse even the best offer. Your partner has the right not to read this book.

Do not, however, interpret your partner's avoidance of activities/ interactions as meaning he or she does not want a close relationship, just as you do. The problem is that neither of you knows how to achieve intimacy. So here's your chance to be a model for your partner as you move through this text. Your partner may notice a change in your behavior, unless you are in the habit of walking around like an ape.

Do not be discouraged if your partner asks you many questions as you try the different ideas recommended in this book. Be prepared to hear from your partner:

"Didn't we try that?"

"Will this work?"

"Why are we doing this?"

"Who told you to do that?"

"Are you serious?"

"When are we going to get better?"

"Is there anything we haven't done?"

"What is so different about this?"

"How can anything work?"

"Have you thought about something else?"

"Where in the world did this come from?"

Questions, questions, questions. Do not be discouraged if you hear any of these questions. For example, if you are asked, "Why should this work when everything else has failed?" your answer is simple: "I want to change myself; I want our relationship to improve our lives." You have not offered information or a confrontation; you have offered hope.

Now, you may get premature anxiety before you try certain things because you fear how your partner will react. Instead of prejudging your partner, simply notice how he or she responds. But there's no need to worry; your sense of humor will protect you from any reaction you fear. And you may be surprised, because if you try the things I recommend, your partner will have no choice but to respond with warmth.

If you do for yourself, your relationship can only benefit. Once you learn Primitive Communication, you set up a safe environment in which your partner can respond in a new, nondefensive way.

So don't be discouraged if you are starting alone. Just don't expect your partner to applaud you. You must applaud yourself. It won't take long for your partner to feel the changes and want to learn more about Primitive Communication.

Seven-Day Warm-Up

Before we get to gorilla-strength Primitive Communication, I want to start you at chimp strength. For that reason, there is a seven-day warm-up—a sort of beginner's exercise program I want you to try. It will introduce you to the primitive way of relating and will prepare you to go on to the major topics covered later in the book. These warm-up exercises give you a chance to practice the basic skills that are the foundation for all the tactics I will ask you to experiment with.

Each day, I'll ask you to spend a few minutes doing a different warm-up. After seven days, you'll have a good sense of how to proceed when you get to the tactics.

You may do these exercises by yourself or with your partner. Remember, do not use the excuse that your partner is not interested. Your partner may become interested if you introduce new behaviors in a warm and loving way. Do not inflict any exercise on your partner. You may offer and see if the offer is accepted. If it is, great. If not, I've already explained the benefits of proceeding on your own. Have fun.

11

WARNING
The following exercises are serious business. They may be simple, but if they are done properly, you will begin to change your behavior in a relationship. It's *not too late to turn back*! Once you flip this page, however, you'll have no choice but to get closer to your partner.

DAY 1

1. Today, make a list of the following words: *what, where, when, who,* and *why.* Carry this list with you and look at these words several times during the day.
2. Look into a mirror and touch your ear, nose, chin, and lips. If your partner is available, he or she can be invited to watch.
3. In your bedroom, for a few minutes, walk like an ape. Bend a little and swing your arms. Your partner may want to mimic your behavior.

Comments: It's great if your partner wants to join you in these exercises, but remember, you can do them by yourself.

If you do these together, you'll have a ball. If you do them by yourself, do not be surprised if you get a few glances from your partner.

DAY 2

1. Rip up the list of words. You've looked at the list—now forget it. From here on, do not use these words with your partner.
2. Touch your ear, nose, chin, and lips, but not silently. Hum while touching. If you can, touch your partner's facial parts and hum.
3. Walk like an ape for three minutes, with or without your partner—make grunts like an ape. Do not use words.

Comments: *Stop asking your partner questions; make statements.*

Get used to touching and making sounds.

You and your partner will learn that not every statement must have a meaning. You can be silly together, have fun, and not know why.

DAY 3

1. Today you get an exemption. You may ask your partner, "How is the weather?"
2. Touch your lips and say, "Lips." Then smack your lips together to make a loud kissing sound. If your partner wants to kiss, you may kiss, but only using loud sounds like an ape.
3. When you talk to your partner, start a few sentences using Me instead of I. You can pick up a banana and say to your partner, "Me love banana."

Comments: *I gave this exemption because I know there will be slips. I know that when you go to a Chinese restaurant you will ask, "Do you want to order from column A or B?" Do try to limit your questions. You could say, "Let's order from column A or B." Thus you avoid the question.*

Imagine two apes kissing. That will give you the right setting for kissing and making sounds.

Welcome to the world of Primitive Communication. Now, that wasn't so hard.

DAY 4

1. Go over to your partner at least twice today and say, "Me no ask questions."
2. You are now ready to touch and talk. Go over to your partner, hug, and say, "Me hug."
3. Begin to start conversations with your partner by using Me. Do this even when you are outside of your home. Today, place one phone call to your partner. Start the conversation with "Me called you. . . ."

Comments: *You have now made a declaration of independence from questions. No more inquisitions, no more cross-examinations. This is a verbal commitment to avoid hostility in your language. Watch your tone as you make statements. Do not set up an ambush by making a simple statement but with a harsh tone. Remember, watch your tonality.*

It takes a lot of courage to be silly, but being serious didn't work—so give this a try.

DAY 5

Today we put it all together.

Embrace, hug, and tap each other lightly while in an embrace, saying, "Me care for you."

You are now not asking questions, you are now touching and talking, and you are now both mature enough to use advanced Primitive Communication.

Comments: You made it. In just five days an offering of intimacy has been made. Nothing complex, just simplicity. Just sharing.

Since Primitive Communication may still sound a bit strange to you, tomorrow I'll give you an exercise to practice some basic words.

DAY 6

Using Primitive Communication will help to reveal your true needs. At the same time your "old system" of disguising your needs with eloquent and intellectual words will diminish.

With practice it is not difficult to pronounce Primitive Communication words, though a great deal of resistance must be overcome. All new languages seem hard at first; the following chart will help you build confidence.

Steps	Pronunciation
1.	Pronounce the letter Y (as in "yellow").
2.	Pronounce the letter U (as in "underwear").
3.	Pronounce the letter M (as in "monkey").
4.	Put it all together and say "YUM."
5.	If you are stuck, pronounce the word "GUM," then substitute the Y for the G.
6.	Say "YUM-YUM."
7.	Now say "YUMMIES" (rhymes with "tummies").
8.	Put it all together and say, "Me give yummies."
9.	Repeat these words to your partner at least three times a day, for about fifty years.

DAY 7

Daily Exercise Reps

On day seven you begin your daily exercise reps, which you should do faithfully until your intimacy muscles are sufficiently developed. If at any point you have a relapse and retreat from intimacy, just come back to the daily reps to regain your muscle tone.

Stand in front of a mirror and go into an ape position. If you do not have confidence, your first exercise should be nonverbal: scratch yourself for a few minutes. After this warm-up you are ready for some simple repetitions:

Level 1. Say Five Times, "Me/ Me." If you are successful with these five reps, you will be ready for a further downgrading of your intellectual self. Level 2 will also upgrade your intimacy level.

Level 2. Say Five Times, "Me and Partner." Do not resist this downgrading. If you do not have the strength for five reps, just do what you can, but keep exercising until you reach this level.

Level 3. At Advanced Level 3, Say Five Times, "Me Need Partner." At first, this level will be quite difficult. This level overcomes several decades of practicing the wrong exercise ("I don't need anyone").

Note: Stay at level 3 for the rest of your life. These daily reps will strengthen your intimacy muscle while at the same time atrophying your intellectual muscle.

PRIMATE FOREIGN PHRASE DICTIONARY

While you are learning Primitive Communication, you can use this foreign phrase dictionary to help you translate the complex words you use every day into Primitive Communication.

I think that the first time I saw you, there was something about your glance that intrigued me.
Me like you.

If there are mutually compatible areas that interface with our interests, we might be able to plan some type of agenda.
We be together.

Sometimes I just stare out into space, knowing that there is a void in my life that can be filled only with intimate contact.
We hug.

I can't believe that you forgot to send me a birthday card on the only day of the year when I expect something from you. You know it's not the gift that has meaning; it is the idea that you took time out to remember.
Me important to you.

Why do you keep asking me questions about what I am thinking?
Me need trust.

I can't remember the last time that you made an uncritical comment about my attitude toward you. When I make a comment about the house being dirty, it is not that I want you to clean each time, because you know that I really share the responsibility for the household, especially the cleaning.
Let's make love.

You keep changing your mind about what you want me to do for you. One day you want this, one day you want that. Each time I talk to you, I don't know if you want this or that.
Notice me.

We have no fun in our lives. Everything we do has to be based on some concrete goal, which must result in our being in a constant state of flux, never being fully settled, and always striving for new acquisitions.

Let's make a malted.

Why are you always on the telephone? I think you have found a perfect way of pretending that you are with me while you are constantly feeding into the troubles of your friends on the telephone.

Feed me.

Don't think I didn't notice you looking at that model in the store window. I saw you touch the window pane. You know that caused me great pain.

Touch me.

I can't stand what we do to each other. Everything we do, everything we say, I feel does not work. I don't know what to do to try to get us back to where we were when we first met.

Me need affection.

Topics, Tactics, and Tasks

The following topics should have meaning for most relationships. You may want to read them sequentially, or you may want to skip around. If you cover one topic that interests you each week, you will be finished in several weeks. I do not think the material should be covered in a few nights, though, because change is not an overnight process. Neither do I think that the material should take a few years. I think that a goal of several weeks is about right to swing a relationship from intimidation to intimacy. In fact, intimidation can be suppressed after a few days. The warm-up should have begun to set a limit on it.

Now gather up your courage and try the many ways of relating that I suggest in the following pages.

Let's bring intimacy into your relationship. Just follow my instructions and feel your pleasure grow.

Topic 1: Problems, Problems, Problems

We come to relationships with many of our ideals, feelings, values, and habits already formed. So, unless you and your mate are perfect (in which case you can put the book down and pat yourselves on the back), you've probably experienced conflict over ideas, feelings, values, and habits. You must take a step back to learn how not to inflict yourself on others and to learn to truly share with others. Here the tactics allow you to take a step back and change your signals to show that you are approachable.

Ideas:	Armor vs. Vulnerability
	Amnesia
	Drama vs. Comedy
	The Why vs. the Way
Tactics:	Being Selfish
	Arrogance
	Expectations
	Judgments
	Slogans
	Interpretations
	Rejection
	Jealousy
	Power Struggle
	Self-Abuse
	SOS
	Complaint Box

Task Menu

IDEAS

Armor vs. Vulnerability

Primitive people were vulnerable to illness and climate because they did not have the protection we do today. As we have become protected by technological armor, we also, unfortunately, have clothed ourselves with psychological armor.

We must now work hard to allow ourselves to experience emotional exposure and vulnerability. We can keep our high-tech protection so we don't have to suffer the exposure to earthly hazards, but we must drop our unhealthy armor of emotional "sophistication."

We know how to fly solo at high altitudes, but now we must learn to crawl with a partner at low altitude. At low altitude, partners do not need complicated compasses in order to navigate their course; they just need to touch (gently guide) each other, and they will go in the right direction.

Amnesia

Amnesia can be a powerful friend in improving a relationship. A partner may remember something from the past that haunts him or her for several decades. To carry a grudge, a vendetta, for a long time can be damaging to a relationship. You must ask yourself, "Does the average gorilla maintain an inventory of unresolved hurts?"

By leaving most grudges behind, you send a message of trust to your partner. Your partner does not remember what was said on a Monday, thirty years ago, at breakfast, while eating a bag of peanuts. Your partner probably remembers the peanuts and not what was said.

Do not thrust a historical hurt down your partner's throat. Do not forget the joy of amnesia. Embrace memory loss in order to avoid the unnecessary pain of retention. Then the archives of hurt can be closed.

Drama vs. Comedy

When couples are in trouble, they tilt toward drama instead of comedy. We must learn to embrace comedy and reject our need to be overly dramatic. The drama of pain and violence is exciting when we think of Ray Milland trying to knock off Grace Kelly or of James Cagney smashing a grapefruit into Mae Clark's face. But the drama can turn into tragedy when a partner decides to do harm. It is a shame that we have adopted so easily the drama of violence.

Partners should get more excited about the comedy of Jane and Tarzan swinging among the trees. How can anyone think of violence when watching Fred Astaire and Ginger Rogers dancing all the way to Rio? We have to learn to replace the violent titillations of Rocky and Rambo with the excitement of Tracy and Hepburn. The comedy of George Burns and Gracie Allen can surely stimulate us to become vigilantes of laughter and closeness, rather than vigilantes of the street. Partners need these visions of comedy.

The Why vs. the Way

When we enter a partnership, we really do not know how to behave. We want our needs to be fulfilled, but we don't know how to get those needs met. Thus, we think it is difficult to learn how to partner, and we try extra hard.

Because we are logical people, we assume that if we work hard to understand the problems in our relationships, our relationships will get better and we'll get our needs met. In short, we think that if we understand the "why" (insight), we will change. Well, sometimes we do change; sometimes we do not. To have insight about why you are feeling rejected in a relationship can immobilize you, which can in turn cause you to hide your feelings in hostile communications toward your partner ("You never hug me").

A "way" (a path to wisdom) is needed, whether or not we know why, because our first priority is to bring about a difference in our behavior. With Primitive Communication, the *way* can mean saying, "Me lonely," a statement very likely to get you the nurturing and love you need— posthaste. With the *way*, you can experience change without understanding the past. And once the *way* has brought about growth and change, you can enjoy the luxury of insight, should you so desire—but moving on to new experiences is a lot more fun.

Freud gave us the *why*. Zen gave us the *way*. Primitive Communication is based on the Zen concept of experience as the ultimate changer and teacher. For it is clear to me that the intellectual knowledge we have obtained about relationships (the *why*), while interesting enough to discuss at psychologists' conferences, may not lead to wisdom. I mean, do you think learning about penis envy helped anyone have better sex? It is our openness to experience (the *way*) that leads to closeness.

So you see, being a good partner is no more difficult than opening yourself up to the experience of closeness through honest, open Primitive Communication. This experience will lead to wisdom (or at least great sex).

TACTICS

Being Selfish

Being selfish is an important part of the coupling process. To be intimate with another person requires that you also be selfish in a healthy way. Once you have taken care of many of your needs, you will find it easier to help another person with his or her needs. It is when a person is not selfish and caters to the other that hostility may become a major theme in a partnership.

When you do something for yourself, tell your partner that you are being selfish. Say to your partner, "Me do for me." Your partner will say, "What about me?" Answer this by saying, "Me happy with me, then me do for you."

To be unhealthy and unselfish means denying your needs; when you are healthy and selfish, you feel more creative and giving. Deprivation will only lead you to be a martyr, finding new and undiscovered ways to suffer.

Comments: *I once worked with a so-called unselfish husband who continually told his wife, "I'm worried about you, I'm concerned about you, I'm anxious about you." I told him that he really didn't care about her because he was always rescuing her and she responded by being an invalid (alcoholic). I tried to get him to use Me in order to expose his feelings and to stop manipulating her to need him as this savior. I wanted him to say, "Me helpless," "Me frightened," "Me vulnerable," "Me exhausted."*

He refused to use Me because he didn't want his wife to think that he was selfish. He also said to me, "I'm worried about your competency." He dropped me as his therapist, and she kept drinking.

31

Arrogance

You may feel that your partner is arrogant just at the time you need him or her. A typical reaction is to disguise your need for your partner because you do not want to plead and beg for attention. You do not want your partner to bring you to your knees. If your disguise is effective, then your partner will also feel ignored. The trick, then, is not letting this situation escalate to jungle warfare.

You must get over this aversion to pleading. Your partner will not bring you to your knees if you first allow *yourself* to get to your knees. When your partner is innocently watching Bugs Bunny on TV, start your pleadings. Get on your knees and say, "Me beg you to need me." Your partner will undoubtedly laugh. Isn't it better to receive a laugh in your face than an arrow in your heart?

Comments: Isn't it amazing that partners can build a home, raise kids, and plan for retirement yet find it difficult to admit a need for each other? This thing called life is such a lonely experience without a special partner to share all of that joy and pain. Primitive Communication helps to return couples to a state of mutual dependence.

Be more independent by admitting this need to be dependent. The statement "Me need you" is a blessed event—you give birth to a mature you by walking away from the adolescent you, who thinks that you can do it alone.

Expectations

It is natural to expect things from others, but if you don't stop expecting so much, then many opportunities for closeness may be lost. Many relationships are destroyed by too many expectations.

Don't say to your partner, "If you don't put that paper down this instant and talk to me, I'll scream!" Your expectation may not be well received. A better statement would be "Me need attention." At least you are sharing your need, but not by demanding.

Your primitive statement will free you from being helpless and will break a negative cycle without your having to slam doors and throw things.

Comments: *I worked with one woman who had a massive expectation problem. Each statement she made was a "request," but she claimed that she was just expressing feelings. In reality, her feelings were really expectations of her partner. The more expectations he heard, the more resistant he became.*

I asked her to substitute Me for I when starting a sentence and to focus on the feeling.

Her so-called feelings would be expressed as "Why don't you bring me flowers? That'll show that you love me." This type of expectation damaged the relationship. I then helped her shift her statement to "Me need flowers—me feel alone."

This technique of primitive language forced feelings out of her, and her husband did not feel attacked or hostile. He began to feel trusted, and a closeness developed.

Judgments

One effective method of destroying a relationship is to engage in judgmentalism. It is OK to share your preferences, but it is not OK to classify your partner with statements involving right or wrong.

You might make a simple statement, but your partner's reaction could be explosive. You might say, "It's better to go to the beach today than tomorrow." Your partner might answer, "If you want heat, then go to hell." Why the explosion? The word *better* is a value judgment about what is right for your partner, but your partner does not want to be told what is better for him or her. Your partner would not explode if you said, "Nice day for beach." Your partner would then be able to decide without dealing with the word *better*.

Many times when you tell a person what is right for him or her, you are really telling your partner what is good for you. Admit what is good for you without being manipulative. Say, "Me prefer this for me." Your partner will feel loved because of your honesty.

Comments: *Classification is a form of manipulation in order to obtain control over your partner. If you classify your partner as sick, lazy, insensitive, or oversexed, then you are inflicting a form of judgment to gain power in the relationship. If too much power is concentrated within one partner, the other may become so enraged as to demand a new classification of the relationship:*

Married
↓
Separated
↓
Divorced

Avoid classification by getting back to basics.

Slogans

Slogans can drive partners nuts.
Be careful if you keep repeating
to your partner:
"The best is yet to come."
"An apple a day keeps the
doctor away."
"Let's go one step at a time."
"Remember the Alamo."
Slogans, besides being trite,
make everything too pat. Life is
full of surprises that slogans
don't account for.
If you're in the habit of
spouting slogans to your partner,
fool him or her when least
expected. If your partner
expects a slogan like "The best
things in life are free," then you
should say instead, "The best
thing in your life is me."

Interpretations

Do not interpret your partner's behavior. You are not an analyst. You must tell your partner how his or her behavior affects you, not what you believe is causing the behavior. Do not say, "You sound angry because you had a bad day at the office."

Shift to a primitive statement that reveals what the anger does to you: "Me feel stressed."

Your partner's anger does cause a stress in you. Your statement forces your partner to focus on your feelings rather than your interpretation.

Keep your analytic couch out of your home, especially the bedroom.

Comments: *Your partner will suffer less if you do not interpret his or her statements; after all, you are not the analyst of the family. You can guess someone else's motivation, but you never really know.*

Rejection

If you feel rejected, don't become a martyr. There are benefits to suffering, but if it becomes a habit, it could last a lifetime. Instead, become a hunter.

What are you going to hunt? Not your partner's head; you are going to hunt for tenderness.

Go to your supermarket, buy a meat tenderizer, and show this to your partner. Say to your partner, "Let's get tender." Your partner will say, "Why?" You say, "We get softer when we get tender."

Your partner will think that you are off the wall; however, your partner will be ready for your next tender move. You won't feel rejected if your partner says, "During lovemaking it is important to be hard instead of soft," and you can say, "Me like you both hard and soft." If you feel exhausted after a while from too much lovemaking, the next time you go to the supermarket, buy some chopped liver.

Comments: I hope by now you've gotten into the habit of:

- *avoiding asking questions*
- *talking while touching*
- *substituting Me for I*

I also hope that you are feeling better about pleasure as a substitute for suffering. If this intimacy is frightening, I am sure that you can slam a judgment on your partner ("I think that you do not love me") in order to again experience the pain that goes with this intimidation.

If you do have a relapse, make it a short one, get back to intimacy ("Me need to feel loved"), pass Go, and collect two hundred kisses.

Jealousy

If you are jealous, do not hide this fact. If your partner admires someone else, he or she also wants to know that you care. By hiding your jealousy, you risk making your partner feel ignored and unloved.

Someone else may be giving your partner extra attention, which makes you uncomfortable. Do not say, "Are you having an affair?" This question could actually encourage an affair because your feelings of insecurity are buried. Say to your partner, "Me jealous. Me love you." This language will pull your partner toward you without making him or her feel intimidated.

Jealousy is a smoke screen for the fear of being abandoned. Be courageous and let your partner know about this fear. If you say, "Please no abandon me," your partner will want to make you feel secure and your jealousy will evaporate. Expressing your vulnerability will lead to safety. Do not be jealous—be vulnerable.

Comments: *I saw one wife who hid her jealousy by questioning her husband about every woman he talked to. She feared that her husband would leave her just as her father had left her mother. She could not express her fear, so she acted jealous.*

She forced her husband to take care of her by getting migraines. This curtailed her jealousy because he was so busy taking care of her. She felt that if he had to take care of her, he would not have time for other women.

Her husband loved her, but he was a nonverbal person and did not express his love. This lack of expression of love only made her more jealous.

I asked her to use Primitive Communication and to say, "Me need to be with you; please no abandon me." I suppressed his answer of "Why do you say that?" and asked him to say, "Me stay with you." This satisfied her need to be wanted and to hear that she was. She got fewer headaches, and he learned to be more expressive. She learned that she did not have to be an invalid or be jealous. The relationship became more meaningful for both.

Power Struggle

The power struggle is a normal occurrence within a relationship. Each partner wants to be in control. This leads to confrontations between partners.

One way to undermine this struggle is to let your partner know that you want to listen to what he or she has to say. Listening is not placating or submitting. You simply say, "Me listening." This sends a signal that what your partner says is important, which reduces the need to be in control.

If the struggle heats up, say, "Me disagree, but me still listen."

It will be difficult for your partner to keep up any confrontation if you are listening. Do not be surprised if your partner says, "Me also listen to you."

Comments: *One husband kept screaming at his wife, "Why didn't you pick up my cleaning?" and her response was to cry. Her crying was a countertactic to repress his screaming at her. That just made him scream more. Instead, I asked her to say, "Me need tickee for shirtee." When she said this, he calmed down because he felt listened to. This suppressed his intimidation tactic of screaming. After this they both laughed and were able to talk simply about the daily household chores.*

Self-Abuse

Often partners resort to self-abuse as a solution to their feelings of insecurity. This self-abuse not only hurts you; it is also a way of abusing your partner, because you stop paying attention to your partner and manipulate him or her into taking care of you.

Instead of being self-abusive, become vocal and absurd. Whip yourself with banana skins and say to your partner, "Me peeling insecure." Your partner will now pay attention to you, even if it's only to throw bananas. Throwing nice things, like pillows, bananas, or kisses, can be a positive way for some partners to try to reach each other.

If vocalization and absurdity do not occur, then the self-abuse can escalate into a confrontation. Asparagus spears are then thrown, and someone could get hurt, so keep it at the banana level.

Comments: *I worked with one couple who were children of alcoholics, and they wrote the book on mutual abuse. They gave each other a daily dose of screaming, slapping, and punching.*

I asked them not to wait to become abusive. I asked them to set an alarm to get up one hour early and throw popcorn at each other.

They became less abusive because they became frustrated at losing the hour's sleep, and they got tired of cleaning up the popcorn. Their absurd behavior reduced their hostility.

SOS

Partners need to learn to recognize distress signals in a family. Save our system (SOS) needs to be signaled in an open way. If you feel the relationship is in trouble, do not assume that your partner also knows. Send up an SOS by saying, "Me sinking in our relationship."

Do not try to hide the fact from your partner that you are drowning. Be honest and tell your partner that you are drowning in the relationship.

If you do not send up a distress flare, do not expect any rescue attempt from your partner.

Comments: *Too many people, after twenty years of marriage, are surprised that their partner wants out. The partner who is leaving never told the other person that he or she was unhappy. It is a sad event for both. Strong signals of dissatisfaction should have been sent. They were not.*

41

Complaint Box

All good jungle outposts have complaint boxes attached to the doorways of the huts. Put one in your house and start all messages with "Me no like _____." It is important for partners to feel that they can complain and be heard.

Both of you should check this box regularly in order to get feedback. For a surprise you might occasionally slip in a love note—it is also important to take a holiday from complaining.

Sometimes we complain not because things are so bad, but because things are going so well. So if you are superstitious, if you find that your partner is getting too relaxed, you can always leave a nasty note in the complaint box.

Comments: *If you are superstitious about good things happening to you, I will now protect you with a mojo:*

Booma-laka, Booma-laka,
Booma-laka, Boom.
Me, the Maniacal one,
Sends message of protection
To readers of this text,
I now warn all evil spirits,
Me give evil spirits the hex.

You are now free to experience pleasure with your partner.

TASK MENU

Since you are religiously doing your daily exercise reps, I know that your intimacy muscle is starting to firm.

This week you should have accomplished at least two of the following:

- Went to the movies and saw some partners in action (Tarzan and Jane, Fred Astaire and Ginger Rogers)
- Gave your partner a meat tenderizer
- Set up a home complaint box
- Threw out all of your pop psychology books
- Forgot about two rotten things your partner did
- Got on your hands and knees—and not just to perform a sexual act
- Listened

I suspect that you were able to do at least two of these tasks from the main menu, either alone or with your partner. As a reward for you, I've got a wonderful dessert treat:

Special Treat Place this book on your kitchen table and tell your partner, "Me learn to be an open book."

Topic 2: Courting

Courting is not just a precommitment process; it is a process that lasts a lifetime. Making another person feel wanted and needed is not a by-product of a relationship; it is the cornerstone of a relationship. When you finally find a partner, you haven't reached the end of courting, but rather the beginning of the real courting process. Whether you're hunting for a future partner or the one you already have, don't hesitate to adapt the ideas and tactics that follow.

Ideas:	On a Relationship Safari
	Smoke Signals
	Weddings and Wedding Nights
	Dating Chart

Tactics:	Hunting for a Partner
	Heartbreak and Risk
	Primitive Courting
	Kissing
	Partner Plumage
	Intimacy Dictionary
	Primitive Poetry
	Feeding
	Spontaneous Contact
	Getting Engaged

Task Menu

44

IDEAS

On a Relationship Safari

Think back to your first romance. You were young, full of energy, and desperately in love. You knew you were just a shell of a person until you met your beloved. He or she alone understood you. You were Romeo and Juliet.

Somewhere along the line (usually after that first breakup) your attitude about relationships changed. You grew up. You realized that you don't really need anyone. Even when you fell in love again, you held back. After all, emotional health in our society is measured by independence. We all go around beating our chests, congratulating ourselves on how strong we are: "Me Tarzan."

Partners must learn the difference between traveling light and traveling alone. If a relationship becomes disposable, then we may throw away everything in order to acquire new partners. This is just as strange as clinging to each other like barnacles. If a relationship becomes nomadic, however, somewhere between these extremes, burdens are lifted and we enjoy each other much more. We retain our independence, but we acknowledge our partners: "Me Tarzan, you Jane."

Relationships exist in a continuum:

Disposable	Nomadic	Too Intense
Abdication	Accommodation	Desperation

Primitive Communication helps partners tilt toward being nomadic and accommodating. To abdicate, to give up, leads to feelings of persecution. To be desperate in love leads to feelings of resentment. To accommodate, to negotiate, leads to feeling protected.

Who wants to go on a safari without feeling protected?

Smoke Signals

We are constantly sending confusing signals to each other, signals that our partners cannot decode. These signals can easily be interpreted incorrectly. A difficult signal to decode is "Do you love me?" It tells nothing about the sender and puts a demand on the receiver.

A simple primitive signal would be much stronger because it avoids the smoke screen effect. Asking for a hug, rather than hiding behind a manipulative question, will bring better results and will make you feel more secure. It is better to say, "Hug-hug." This primitive signal cannot be misinterpreted. It has the power of a jungle drumbeat.

Weddings and Wedding Nights

Too many couples worry about "keeping up with the Joneses" when planning a wedding. The cost of a wedding can be quite prohibitive when you add up the cost of the hall, catering, music, flowers, etc. Your bill can run to several thousand dollars.

Forget about the Joneses; think about keeping up with the Tarzans. Your wedding can be held at a friend's hut, and you can serve fruits and vegetables. Rent a radio and even wear a rented hula skirt. Don't give the ushers and bridesmaids expensive gifts; give them pineapples. This type of wedding should cost a few hundred dollars. Even if you don't go all the way with the ape theme, remember the purpose of the event. This is more than a birthday or bar mitzvah for two.

The wedding night should be different, too. Counting cash and candy dishes has occurred on the traditional wedding night. Lovemaking may also occur if not much cash is given. Instead, treat yourself to a motel that has a VCR and bring along a Tarzan film. Let your mind be influenced by the simplicity of language between Tarzan and Jane. Look at each other and grunt; your night of romance will be memorable. Isn't this a better idea than talking about which table your relatives sat at and whether the meat was well done? It is more important for romance that you be well done.

Dating Chart

To employ Primitive Communication at the courting stage means following a new sequence instead of the typical dating pattern. This chart can act as a guide. This sequence—indeed, dating in general—is also great for couples who have been together a long time but are renewing their relationship with Primitive Communication.

	Typical Sequence	**PC Sequence**
First Date	Ask questions.	Share bananas.
Second Date	Make premature commitment.	Hold hands at zoo.
Third Date	Make love.	Hold hands while watching a Tarzan film.
Fourth Date	Make love.	Buy matching loincloths.
Fifth Date	Power struggle over: Commitment Abandonment Control	Embrace in front of local fruit store.
Sixth Date	Break up.	Discuss the possibility of making love, but more important, share a mashed banana. This sharing leads to a feeling of security.
Rest of Life	Wonder what went wrong.	Continued growth, love, and fun. Feelings about abandonment and control rarely get to the point where the relationship is threatened.

TACTICS

Hunting for a Partner

Dogs, cats, and inflatable rubber dolls are not partners. These are pets. These pets may lick some of the problems of isolation, but you need a partner if you want to be in a relationship.

It is OK to advertise for a partner. But when you write an ad for your local paper, don't be too sophisticated. "Bright single violinist wishes to meet a literate and sensitive pianist in order to create beautiful new music" is witty, but you might lose many potential partners because they are intimidated.

Your ad should be primitive:

Desperately seeking a lover of bananas, coconuts, and prunes. Would love to dance to sound of drums and swing from trees. If you go ape over jungle serenades, please send me bongo beats.

You will be swamped with replies.

Even if you have been in a marriage for thirty years, you can let your partner know that you are still hunting for him or her by placing a personal ad in your local newspaper proclaiming that your partner is your sweetheart.

Comments: It is difficult to let others know that you want to reach out. So many of us hide this fact by pretending that we can make it alone. Have the courage to let others know you are available, either to attract a partner or to keep attracting the partner you have.

Heartbreak and Risk

During courting, each partner wonders who will be the first to take a risk. Have the courage to go first. Say, "Me take risk on you."

If your partner runs, then you found out early in the game. It is not a bad thing to be rejected by someone who is not open to fun and growth. If your partner stays, he or she will not ask you why you use poor grammar but will admire you instead for having the courage to take the risk.

We now have a good beginning.

Comments: *If you go for intimacy, then you do risk having your heart broken. If you do not take this risk, you have to go through months and years of testing each other. The testing process can destroy a relationship.*

Do not test the other person. Instead, test yourself to see how many ways you can use the language of intimacy to open yourself up. This is an invitation for your partner to reciprocate.

Primitive Courting

Return to an age of elegance by engaging in primitive courting. Celebrate your relationship by symbolically showing your partner that he or she is special. Each day for a full week, bring a different vegetable—a radish, a tomato, then celery, and, of course, a cucumber. As you offer these treats, tell your partner, "You are special."

Primitive courting may not be received at first as a romantic gesture. Your partner may think that you have become as soft as a tomato between the ears. Just assure him or her that you have; this judgmental feeling will pass when your partner hears that he or she is special.

Your courting will reap many rewards. Your partner, in a fit of passion, will probably tell you that *you* are special and bring you a romantic treat—maybe a banana shake. Primitive elegance has its rewards.

Kissing

Kissing is a wonderful way of having fun. It is also a lost art form.

Kissing as a form of touch has been too often associated with sexuality. It also should be associated with fun and affection.

Go to your partner, pucker your lips, let out some smacking sounds, and say, "Me give you ape kiss."

Your partner may think you are initiating sex, but you can laugh and kiss him or her again and show that you are offering fun and affection. Once the kiss is accepted for what it is, you will both be delirious with the taste of closeness. You have just brought back a lost art.

Partner Plumage

Your partner needs to be noticed, and it is your job to do the noticing. When your partner dresses up to show you his or her new plumage, don't wait to be asked, "What do you think of this new hat?" Be assertive; go to your partner and say, "Nice hat."

Go over and touch the hat; also touch some hair. While stroking your partner's hair, don't be afraid to touch an ear or a chin. The plumage was placed there to get your attention. While stroking, also admire the parts you are touching by stating, "Nice ear, nice nose, nice chin."

Your partner will feel noticed and flattered. Be careful not to ask how much the plumage cost. Your partner may interpret this as encouragement to ask someone else to stroke his or her chin. And how would you feel if your partner gave good chin to someone else?

Comments: By noticing your partner, you will make him or her feel loved. You also signal your own vulnerability to his or her attractiveness. These acts of vulnerability help a relationship work.

Intimacy Dictionary

Partners need to have fun with words. With your partner, start an Intimacy Dictionary (ID). Enter into the ID words that are exclusive to your partnership.

Example: "Lube Job" means "Lovemaking."

If the next time your partner says, "Me need lube job," you do not remember the meaning of these words, tell your partner, "Just a second; me get ID."

That's the right answer.

Be silly with words. It breeds intimacy.

Primitive Poetry

Rekindle your literary urges by writing primitive poetry to your partner:

My darling Dick
when I am sick,

I know we click
'cause we are slick,

Together we are chic
'cause my heart goes tic-tic-tic.

How overjoyed your partner will be upon receiving this poem. Just imagine your partner saying to you, "Darling, what a lovely poem, but my name is Harold."

Comments: I love to encourage partners to play with words. With the right words you can't stop intimacy.

If I meet resistance to saying, "Huggy-poo," then I'll say, "OK, as long as we end our statement with poo, we can use something more sophisticated, like Sigmund Freud-poo." This switch often stops resistance because we all really want to use and hear words of affection.

Me grateful these words are being read. Thanks-poo.

Feeding

We go to elegant restaurants for both food and socialization. This is an expensive type of interpersonal contact that many times leaves us emotionally empty.

Get a wooden bowl and use your fingers to feed your partner. (With soup, feed your partner directly from the bowl.) Don't be afraid to make a mess.

Make simple sounds when feeding and eating: "Mm—food and fingers, mm—good, good."

You will both feel close because of this feeding. This is one of the benefits of being a slob.

Comments: *Though we should all have the experience of being fed and fussed over as a child, some of us did not. This sharing of food removes feelings of deprivation and substitutes security. When couples feed each other, they share laughter; it is difficult to remain angry.*

When you do this, clear your mind of clutter. Do not think. Allow yourself to nurture someone else and allow yourself to be taken care of.

Spontaneous Contact

Plan an obscene phone call to your partner.

On the phone say to him or her, "I can't tell you my name, but I love that muscle between your legs."

Then hang up. Your partner will feel loved.

Comments: *I absolutely broke up when one of my clients told me she'd called her husband, a high-powered executive, at work. She didn't realize that someone other than her husband had answered her call. Her "obscene" statement was "Tonight, I intend to serve your rooster."*

Her husband found the following telephone message on his desk, "Your wife called—tonight's dinner is chicken."

Don't let this discourage you. Try for that loving call, because it will make your partner feel wanted. Just make sure you recognize his or her voice before you start to speak.

Getting Engaged

Before a commitment, so many partners get caught up in the cost of the engagement gift. Saving for a ring can dominate a relationship. Later, couples agonize over birthday presents, Christmas gifts, or the number of diamonds in the anniversary ring.

You do not need an expensive gift to consecrate your love. Almost anything will do. Choose something that will symbolize the commitment rather than be a financial investment.

Get engaged with a primitive thing. This thing does not have to be a diamond that "lasts forever." Get a wooden ring, which (if you're really hard on it) will last about seventy-five years. Carve your initials in the ring and say to each other, "Our wooden ring will never splinter, nor will we."

You will both feel the pleasure of a commitment without worrying about how much to insure the ring for.

Comments: *I once met a couple who saved for two years in order to buy a ring. When I interviewed each partner individually, I found out that each wanted to save for a down payment on a home but was too afraid to disappoint the other. When they discovered the truth, they bought a less expensive ring and put the rest of the money in a house fund.*

TASK MENU

Remember, if you get a little flabby around the intimacy muscle, you always have the daily exercise reps.

I hope that you made at least two obscene phone calls to your partner this week. If you didn't, get to the phone immediately.

I also hope that you were motivated to do at least two of the following:

- Took a risk by allowing yourself to be vulnerable with your partner.
- Pretended that you just met each other and asked for a date.
- Admired your partner.
- Bought a wooden bowl and poured soup into it, then fed each other.
- Placed a primitive poem on your partner's pillow.
- Pretended to get engaged and gave each other a surprise gift.

Since I'm beginning to have confidence in you, there is no reason I should withhold my special treat for you.

Special Treat Get a scrapbook, and in it start pasting pictures of the two of you. Write on the title page, "Our Romantic Adventure." It will be a treat to see this book develop into a bestseller.

Topic 3: Daily Living

So many couples love each other but have trouble living together. Our daily routines, which may be comfortable to us, can become a burden to others. The tactics in this section help to alleviate some of our day-to-day problems in order to lift this burden.

Ideas: Selective Sharing
Defeating Eloquence
Diagnosis vs. Prescription
Drugs
Anatomy and Language Chart

Tactics: Advanced Telecommunications
Play
Exercise
Napping Without Guilt
Education
Fear of Fun
The Library
Shower and Bath
Cosmetics
Arguments
Messages
Gift Giving
Caretaking

Task Menu

IDEAS

Selective Sharing

Some people really throw themselves into their work, giving their career 100 percent of their time, energy, and emotion. They live to work, and at the end of the day, there doesn't seem to be anything left for their partners. Their careers, quite literally, get the best of them.

Your partner deserves a piece of you, too. If you're saving all of your best jokes and flashiest smiles for your clients or coworkers, you've got to stop being such a pervert. Don't waste all of your charm on others. They can't reward you with goodies as your partner can.

Furthermore, leave your vocational skills at the office. Sure, prosecuting a criminal, selling real estate, and flying an airplane all require skill. But your partner is not your client, customer, or passenger.

You can share feelings with your partner that you would not want to share at the office. You will be a great partner, if, when you are feeling affectionate, you say, "Let's rub coconuts." However, this is not a good thing to say to your clients.

Defeating Eloquence

Each day when you wake up, you talk to yourself: "Oh, God, it's morning already." You then talk to your partner and then to other people around you.

Most people use words to do more than convey simple messages. We use words to try to make ourselves look smart ("This study will impact on all our constituent bases") or to make others look dumb ("Why did you choose *that* one?"). We also use words to mask our actions and our feelings, even from ourselves ("John just isn't right for me") or to manipulate ourselves and others ("Don't you think pink's preferable?"). It's tempting to hide behind words—especially fancy ones—because we can use them to avoid problems, to get what we want from others, and to hide our real feelings.

Be simple in your language. Defeat eloquence and give up this control/manipulation mechanism. If you think that you do not impress others when you do not use eloquence, you are wrong. Your partner and others will be impressed when you do not try to control their behavior.

The fact that you use simple language does not mean that you are a simple person. Simple language means that you want to let others be close to you—now, that's impressive.

Diagnosis vs. Prescription

If you see your partner doing something "wrong," you may be tempted to "diagnose" his or her problem: "You're just like your mother. Every time you say something, it sounds as if you're whining. You learned it as a child, and you should grow up and learn to talk without all of this hysteria."

Even if your diagnosis is correct, your partner does not want to be treated as a patient and may attack you by whining more, offering a few diagnoses of your problems, or saying, "If you treat me as a patient, you should also send me a prescription and a bill." Your diagnosis has created a new problem.

Instead, forget the diagnosis and go straight for the prescription. Touch your partner and say, "Me touch you." This leads to a cure.

You may be concerned about what prompted the whining, but it's probably clear to you by now that you can't undo all of your partner's hurt. At least by touching, you are not perpetuating the problem. You are giving attention, and this is the solution. Your partner's mother may have been a whiner, but by touching, you will be a winner.

Drugs

Drugs create an illusion of freedom, but they are really a trap that snares and disables the user. If you use drugs—from cigarettes to cocaine—then you qualify as a space cadet.

If your partner uses drugs, don't be cool and accept his or her behavior. Become hysterical, make sounds, lose your ability to use words, and most of all, lose your intellectual ability. Do not think that talk and insight will help a drug user.

If you are both users, show this page to someone you trust and beg that person for help. If you decide to do nothing, go to your local zoo and ask the monkeys to make room in their cage.

Try to get your partner off drugs and into Primitive Communication by showing him or her how to get a real high from intimacy. Maybe you want to give your lover a banana peel inscribed with *The Real High Can Be Found Within Our Skin.* Show your partner that when you allow someone to care for you, you do not need an artificial crutch.

Anatomy and Language Chart

Anatomy	Typical Language	Primitive Language
Hand	Would you like to hold hands?	Me feel goo-goo when we hold hands.
Shoulder	You should hug me more often.	Me give huggy-poo.
Hair	Do you mind if I stroke your hair?	Me love to mush up hair.
Stomach	Your stomach feels soft.	Me kiss tummy.
Chest	Is it all right if I touch your chest?	Me nap on chest.
Groin	We certainly need to explore each other's peaks and valleys.	Me feel at home.

TACTICS

Advanced Telecommunications

Partners never seem to have time for each other because they are so "busy." Yet they spend four hours a day watching TV. This TV time causes brain erosion and leaves no time for sharing—even for small talk.

In order to counter this media immobilization, it is important for partners to invest in an advanced telecommunication machine known as the radio.

Begin to withdraw slowly from TV addiction: the slow reduction will prevent withdrawal symptoms—TV tremors. Begin to play music on the radio and talk to each other; say to your partner, "We listen and we talk." Help each other through the TV withdrawal stage.

You will both be happy when you are hooked on radio. Play some old-fashioned tunes and say to each other, "We on same wavelength."

Comments: *Recently, I worked with a couple who could not find any time to talk to each other. It turned out they just watched TV as a way to avoid each other. I recommended a break from the TV by listening to the radio; this could give them a chance to talk.*

At first I was fooled, because they listened to the radio with headphones and managed not to talk.

My second recommendation was that they listen to the radio and dance. They played rock and roll and danced in separate rooms. Still no talking.

I then gave them my best shot: I recommended that they play Hawaiian music and place a lei around each other. They were to whisper, "Me place lei around you." When I met with them the following week, I asked if they had talked. They said no! In fact, they were honest and shared the fact that they had plotted to defeat me. This plotting occurred during the Hawaiian dance. What they forgot, however, was that all the time they were plotting against me they were talking more than they had in years!

Play

For many of us, passive viewing is our only form of play. We read thrillers and romance novels. We go to the movies, and through the fantasy of the cinema we destroy a few people or a few villages, we fall in love, we find meaning in life.

Start to enjoy the experience of life by learning the joys of primitive play. Primitive play is anything that brings a smile to your face without stressing you out—building a model airplane, making clothes for a doll, playing Chinese checkers, or going to your local playground and sitting in the sandbox.

Simple gadgets are important for partners when engaging in play. Although VCRs and computers are important to us, perhaps we should again learn to play with simple toys. Partners can talk and laugh while playing Monopoly, learning the abacus, or body painting each other.

Bring your partner a gift, such as Parcheesi, and play together. Or better yet, when was the last time you played strip poker with your partner? Consider bringing home clay and saying to your partner, "We play with clay." Shape the clay to represent the best part of your partner's body.

Comments: *You can't count on fun to happen by chance. While there are so many areas of your life that can be infused with fun, they are by no means a sure thing. You must plan for fun the same way you plan for any other important part of your life.*

Exercise

Exercise has become a major part of the health improvement movement. Exercise can be more fun if partners exercise together. This could mean swimming, jogging, tree swinging, or advanced banana throwing.

Besides the physical aspects of exercise, these activities also improve a relationship. Say to your partner, "We jump rope." Your partner will say, "Go jump yourself." You should answer this by saying, "Me jump you." After your partner smiles, you may have to negotiate a different exercise—horizontal weight lifting. In the meantime, go for a walk and talk.

Exercising together leads to intimacy and closeness. The couple that sweats together sticks together.

Napping Without Guilt

Partners need to learn to do nothing; always doing something is too fatiguing. Animals do not look at a watch to determine nap time, and humans must learn to shift to a prone position and nap without guilt.

Napping together is an intimate act that reduces stress within the individual and between partners. At first you might be embarrassed to suggest a nap because your partner may be busy with some major scientific advance. Go with your instinct and say, "We nap together." Your partner will look at you in a state of shock and say, "How can you ask me to give up precious time when the world is waiting for my scientific breakthrough on reducing stress?" The shock will pass, and within seconds you should try again. No matter how resistant your partner is, eventually he or she will give in.

When you are napping, a closeness will occur that enhances the relationship. At this time there will be less stress between you—A Major Scientific Breakthrough.

Comments: Partners should help each other clear their minds and reduce the tensions of daily living.

There are many ways to reduce stress; one of the best is the ritual of resting together. When resting together, touch and make soft sounds, or jungle sounds, to let the other know that you are there. This creates a feeling of safety.

When you engage in tension reduction, your partner will live longer, you will live longer, and the relationship will live longer.

Education

Couples begin their real education after they have received their formal degrees and credentials.

For example, if you are thinking of buying a house, why not learn carpentry or gardening together? Buy your partner (and yourself) a book on flowers. When you are ready, buy tools and seeds. Say to your partner, "We water petunias." Together, get your hands dirty and begin the process of learning.

If you learn together, you will make fewer mistakes.

If you bring home a sex manual, don't say to your partner, "This will help you." Instead, say, "We water petunias."

Fear of Fun

If you or your partner is superstitious, you may have a fear of having fun. There may be fear that you're "too old" to engage in pleasure. Say to your partner, "Me fear fun. Me need us to jump up and down, make funny faces, bang pots and pans, and chase evil spirits away."

Your partner will burst out laughing. Appreciate this support from your partner and say, "Me cured."

This is a good start because you have shared your fear.

Comments: *Too many partners are afraid to admit this fear of having fun. It's been so long since they had it that they wouldn't recognize it. And what happens if you have fun and—God forbid—want more!*

The Library

Partners should visit the public library together regularly. It costs nothing, and it helps the partnership. Next time you both look at each other and say, "What should we do?" say, "We go to library."

At the library, browse through newspapers, look at jungle books, and read about different topics; for example, retiring in Bora Bora, tent design, or geriatric birth control. If you see an interesting book, go to your partner and whisper, "Nice book binding; we are also bound."

When partners learn to bind together, intimacy starts to develop. When a partnership is in trouble, partners do not feel bound—they feel isolated. Your words show that you are there for your partner. To be bound does not mean that you are trapped; it means that you recognize the importance of your partner. This may be whispered in the library, but it should also be shouted in the privacy of your jungle hut.

Shower and Bath

It is important for couples to bathe together sometimes. It is fun, and it brings you closer together. (If your bath will hold only one, there is nothing wrong with a shower for two.)

The next time your partner says, "I'm going to take a shower," I want you to say to your partner, "Me shower with you."

If your partner says yes, then you will experience the pleasure of having your back washed. It's only a short distance to your front.

Comments: I have met only one couple who understood the importance of having a large bathtub. They designed a house, and both agreed that the tub should be able to hold two elephants.

These partners were international travelers, and they saw firsthand how different cultures emphasize the importance of a communal-type bath. I take my shower cap off to them.

Cosmetics

We are drowning in perfumes, shampoos, deodorants, and scented soaps. These items are supposed to improve our self-image and make us more attractive to our partner.

These high-tech lubricants are expensive, and they may hide the real person in us. Try to attract your partner with Jungle Juice instead.

Buy some "Pulsating Papaya Juice." Put your fingers into this seductive juice and rub it behind your ears. Say to your partner, "Please lick ears."

Your partner will then state, "You taste like a papaya." To be compared to a papaya is a form of flattery.

If you continue using the high-tech lubricants, you may actually be adding repellents to your body. Go the way of the jungle and start to use things that allow your partner to taste *you*.

Arguments

In order to argue less, you should plan a few arguments a week with your partner. That way you can learn the difference between a good argument and a bad argument.

Examples of how to start a bad argument:

"Why did you say that?"

"Why do you keep scolding?"

"Don't you realize what you are doing?"

Examples of how to start a good argument:

"Me upset."

"Me rejected."

"Me no want to swing from the same tree with you."

Comments: Let's say you plan an argument over who will take out the garbage. First of all, do not ask the question "Who's going to take out the garbage?" Start your argument with "Me tired of taking out garbage." Your partner probably will respond with "Me also tired." The next step is to say, "We take garbage together, then we go take nap." You have now gotten the garbage out of your fights as well.

Messages

Your telephone message recorder should be used to help your relationship. If your message is dull, change it. Make it brief, simple, and caring. Record, "Me not here right now, but me hear message after the beep."

When your friends call, they will think that you have lost it. When your partner calls, you will hear a loving message, "Me miss you," and will leave a loving message in return.

If you don't have a message machine, you can leave love notes for each other—on the refrigerator, under the pillow, on the inside of the toilet lid.

Don't worry about your public; worry about your partner.

Comments: *I know I've told you to keep your Primitive Communication private, but I need you to make an exception here because the wrong phone messages can do so much damage. Use the message above as a benchmark; you might not want to go as far, but your message should be as warm.*

I had a problem with a couple. I just could not figure out why they kept leaving each other abusive messages. They actually had fights over the telephone this way. I finally asked them to bring in their tape messages because I wanted to listen to a fight.

I did not have to listen to the fight. The problem was in the husband's outgoing message, which sounded like the beginning of a corporate board meeting. He stated, "Although I am not in, this machine will record your message, the time you called, and any follow-up action as required by you or me."

When his wife heard this message, she attacked. The only follow-up action she wanted was to hurt him, because she felt hurt by his corporate behavior toward her.

I had him change the message to "Me not home, but if you leave message, me call back."

When she heard the new message, she relaxed and began to leave very loving messages.

Gift Giving

Giving to each other has been translated in our society as "gift giving." To show your love, give a diamond, or a car or a fur or a Rolex. We must reinterpret this consumer ethic as a mandate to give each other the gift of nurturing.

Nurture your partner by:

1. Asking your partner if you may shampoo his or her hair. Then, when your partner is in the bath, surprise your loved one with a very expensive gift: a rubber duck.
2. Offering to give your partner a foot rub. Feel free to use lotion, but only if you don't plan on sucking any toes.
3. Buying matching pajamas.

Comments: *I recently heard from an intellectually gifted couple I had counseled. We had worked hard to downgrade their verbal ability to intimidate each other. They sent me a copy of their wedding vows. How wonderfully primitive they were:*

> We,
> Sweethearts
> of one another,
> Take one another
> for who we are
> Each
> and for who
> we will be
> Together.

With Primitive Communication their verbal intimidation had turned into simple affection.

They had learned to nurture each other.

Caretaking

Of course you feel sad when your partner feels lousy and is in bed with the flu. You will serve your partner tea and sympathy, maybe even a nice piece of toast. Besides this required food ritual, why not cheer up your partner with a tribal dance and chant?

Change your clothes—off with your work clothes. You probably don't have a loincloth, so your best pajamas will do. Dance around the bed and chant, "Boo on the flu." Your partner will state that you are nuts but will smile and feel loved.

Be careful not to dance without clothing, because your partner may become excited and get up before it's wise.

Comments: *We cover up our fear of being alone in many ways. When we get sick, our fear can intensify. If you try to get your partner to analyze this fear, he or she will probably get worse. This intense fear can be broken with Primitive Communication.*

When your partner is ill, touch your partner and say, "Me here for you." Me bring you juice. Me touch you. Me protect you."

When you stroke your partner with loving language, he or she can relax. This language is as powerful as that potent antibiotic, chicken soup. It is not a bad idea to nurture your partner this way even if he or she is not sick.

TASK MENU

By now your intimacy muscles are becoming firmer. You probably love running to a mirror and saying, "Me learning." With this confidence building, I'm certain that you were able to tell your partner that you wanted to nap together. I certainly hope that you were able to do at least three of these tasks:

- Tossed out all nonessential drugs.
- Placed a radio in your bedroom and danced with your partner.
- Took a nap together.
- Bought a petunia plant for your partner.
- Had a good argument.
- Changed the tape on your answering machine.
- Gave a foot rub.
- Went to the library and took out an exercise book.
- Took a bath together.
- Bought matching pajamas.

Just for buying pajamas, you are going to get the following treat.

Special Treat Don't tell anyone about this. After you buy matching pajamas, throw away the bottom halves. You can tell your partner that you bought them at a closeout, but do not reveal the fact that I told you to do this. This is our secret.

Topic 4: Sexuality

Primitive Communication, because it brings about closeness, can allow more—and better—sexual contact. Even if your sex life is already fantastic, you'll find suggestions here that can give it another dimension.

Ideas: Sexuality and Power
Disposability
Lovemaking Sequence Chart

Tactics: Protect Your Mattress
Good Tucking
Deprivation
Primitive Fashion
Compliments
Bargaining
Language and Sexuality
Partner Celibacy
Screaming
Fantasy
Toolbox
Avoid Perversion
Adultery Without Sex
Musical Excitation

Task Menu

IDEAS

Sexuality and Power

Even sexual contact can be more of a power manipulation than an intimacy exchange. If one partner needs to feel more powerful (in control), he or she could use sex to control and manipulate the other person.

With Primitive Communication, partners transmit vulnerability signals. Primitive Communication makes each partner feel needed, and this reduces the need for manipulative behaviors. If you say, "Me need you," the sexual contact becomes an act of equality rather than an act of control.

Disposability

We turn on the TV, and our heroes joke about their latest divorces. The public is encouraged to think about relationships as being disposable, not durable. Feeling low? Get a new coat, a new car, or a new partner. We are taught to crave things, to crave change. If something breaks, we replace it without trying to fix it. This is madness. The media jungle is dangerous.

To overcome this plastic insanity, we must learn to crave less and save more. We must learn that fantasizing about expensive new perfumes and the latest turbocharged cars can disable us. We must turn toward the excitement of primitive dreams and fantasies, which can be forever new if we know how to use them.

Our ever-changing society represses our sexual dreams with visions of "the latest" fashion, trend, or bit of information. We must be strong enough to figure out what we're really buying when we buy into this "disposability" charade: an advertiser's dream.

Since we're not sure of who we are, or what we want, we let others decide for us. Unsure of where you're going? Buy an expensive sports car instead. Or a diamond necklace. Get a divorce. Are these really what we want? Probably not. We probably want to be close to our partners. We probably want sex.

Lovemaking Sequence Chart

Step	Typical Sequence	Primitive Sequence
1.	Quiet French kiss	Noisy ape kiss
2.	Kiss ears	Salivate on slacks (drool)
3.	Fondle top	Pound chest and scream like a gorilla
4.	Fondle bottom	Place nose on navel
5.	Enter-course	While hugging say, "We hug."
6.	Orgasm	Squeeze fresh orange juice
7.	Smoke cigarette	Touch toes and explore partner from head to foot

TACTICS

Protect Your Mattress

When you go to bed at night, you and your partner may have too many people in bed with you. There may be grandfathers, grandmothers, fathers, mothers, and some ex-husbands and ex-wives. The mattress cannot take this pressure. Say to your partner, "Me sleep with only you. Me say bye-bye to old ghosts."

When you get old ghosts out of bed, the mattress will last a lifetime.

Comments: *A partnership is in trouble when each partner keeps accusing the other:*

"You're as crazy as your mother."

"Your father can't talk, and you are just the same way."

Keep these accusations out of the partnership. Focus on sleeping with each other, not with old ghosts.

Good Tucking

No, you didn't read that wrong. It is important for partners to get into good tucking. As children we loved to be tucked in by a parent. Partners need to repeat this act. It makes us feel secure, and it is fun.

At bedtime, pull the covers around your partner and say, "Me tuck you in." Your partner will appreciate it and will rest well.

Comments: I worked with one couple who were so anxious about satisfying each other sexually that it caused tensions. They discussed getting separate beds so they could at least get some sleep.

I asked them to have fun at bedtime, using Primitive Communication while tucking each other in. I asked them to use different tucking phrases each night.

They were both creative and began to have fun with this idea. They tucked each other in and said:

"Me tuck you good."

"Me cover you with affection."

"Me surround you with me."

"Me give you best tuck of your life."

"Me blanket you with love."

The act of tucking led to fun, and this reduced their performance anxiety about sex.

Good tucking led to other good things.

Deprivation

If you are feeling sexually deprived, it is important that you signal your partner about this deprivation. Do not say, "We haven't made love for several decades." If you say this, your partner will probably say, "That's not such a long time." You need to say in a subtle and unobtrusive way, "My petunia needs watering" and point to that spot between your legs.

It will be a hopeful sign if your partner moves toward you with a "watering can." It is a signal that the waiting is over. If your partner moves toward you with a machete with the intent of cutting crabgrass, then for the time being it is better for you to water yourself.

Comments: *One woman told me that her boyfriend was mute. He did not talk before, during, or after lovemaking. I explained to the boyfriend that he might be a great lover but that he was extremely dumb when it came to showing his feelings of affection. Because she threatened to leave the relationship, he was willing to learn.*

I told him that I would teach him the greatest secret of lovemaking and that he was to practice this for fifteen minutes every night. He was to hug his girlfriend, slightly pat her on the back, and say, "Me give huggy-poo." I was willing to share this secret of huggy-poo because, as I told him, he was now emotionally ready.

Each night as he did this, she felt less of a sense of deprivation, and he showed her that he could become verbally articulate. I then taught him more primitive phrases, such as "Me touch," "Me feel," "Me like," and last but not least, "Me love."

This sharing of language helped him begin to share his love. She felt a sense of love and decided to stay in the relationship because she did not feel abandoned anymore.

I hope that you will also try huggy-poo; it works like magic.

Primitive Fashion

If you are feeling ignored, wear your partner's garments—try on his boxers or her flannel nightie. Be silly. No costume is too strange for you to share.

If you want to stay with your gender, don't be misled into buying the most expensive garment on your block. Men don't need to buy the latest bikini shorts from France; just put on a fur hat from Mongolia and nothing else. As you walk into your bedroom, scream, "Me protect you from barbarians."

Ladies can cast aside their sexiest teddies and just wear an old sweatshirt. Write the word FARMER across the shirt. As you walk into the bedroom, say, "It is ten o'clock. Do you know where your cucumber is?"

These clothing symbols will amuse your partner. He or she will respond to your sartorial splendor with love and kindness, if only to stabilize your vulnerable brain.

Comments: *It is important to promote yourself. When exposing your body to your partner, you build trust by not hiding under layers of clothing.*

I once encouraged a husband to promote himself to his wife. Lovemaking occurred only in total darkness, and this upset his wife. He refused to show her his Private Parts. I raised his rank and told him to wear a shirt inscribed with "Major Parts." After all, a major is higher than a private. I think my suggestion went to his head, because he kept the lights on and wore a shirt inscribed with "General Parts." What ego.

Compliments

Partners need to hear that they are desired. Do not be afraid to pay a compliment. When your partner least expects it (when visiting Aunt Matilda and Uncle Murray), lean over and whisper, "Me love your long juicy tongue."

Your partner may look disgusted, but he or she will get excited.

Don't let Matilda and Murray hear this, because they will both go into heat.

Comments: *Couples are reluctant to compliment each other. Couples are not reluctant to be critical. Still, over the years I have heard some wonderful compliments:*

"Over the years, you've become my best friend."

"You grow more beautiful as the years go on."

But these compliments are quite rare because partners are reluctant to reveal such thoughts. Have courage and reveal your complimentary thoughts.

Bargaining

Learning how to bargain sexually leads to more intimate contact. Each partner becomes less fearful. Say to your partner, "Me learning to bargain sexually. Me go with you to visit your aunt three times. Me would love one oral sex session." Your partner will then say, "You are no sexual bargain."

You may interpret this as a hostile statement, but do not overreact. Show you can negotiate. Say, "OK, me go to auntie four times, and me would love to do oral sex only once in front of auntie."

Your partner will now sit you down and put a cold compress on your head. You will receive a hug from your partner. You are both learning how to bargain.

Comments: *Bargaining is a form of economic activity. The marketplace (the bedroom) is full of supply and demand.*

In one couple I saw, the wife did not want to be touched. She felt that sexual contact was an invasion. The more she resisted, the more rejected her husband felt and the stronger his demands became. I explained to the husband that he should signal he wanted to protect his wife by saying, "Me protect you." She then felt he was willing to negotiate, and she allowed him to protect her. Once she felt safe and protected, she became more open to sexual contact.

Language and Sexuality

Sex is just another form of communication. A penis is similar to a microphone, the vagina analogous to a pair of lips. If communication is poor, then sex is usually inadequate. To improve sexuality, communication must first be improved. It's fun for a couple to recognize this relationship between sexuality and language. Write memos to each other. For example: "Loose lips sink ships." "Raise the microphone."

Comments: *A couple who work as therapists are usually the most difficult couple to treat. They ask each other so many questions that they do not have time to make love.*

I found one therapist couple so difficult that I just ordered them to stop talking and thinking before bedtime. They were so busy questioning each other that they avoided making love at all costs.

Finally, I had them write a memo to each other before bedtime:

Me therapist.
Me too smart to make love.

It worked.

Partner Celibacy

If the sexual arena has become part of your power struggle, or if things aren't going well (as in your partner just said, "Don't touch me"), you may want to consider celibacy.

Celibacy helps you take a step back. Say to your partner, "We celibate."

Now physical contact will not be used to hide feelings of insecurity. Begin to talk about the joy of talking. While talking, do not become intellectual and examine what went wrong. Say, "Me miss you" and "Me like your nose" and "Me like your tongue." You may never have told this partner or any partner that he or she has a beautiful tongue.

This period of celibacy should last for about three hours. If you want, you may celebrate the end of celibacy by going to a pet store and watching the rabbits.

Comments: *So many couples complain, "We have sex, but there is no passion." Passion will not return with new sexual positions, but if you reposition your words, then sexuality can return with a passion.*

It is not passionate to ask your partner, "Do you want to make love?" That's a question, and you will probably just get information in return. It is better to state, "Me kiss your coconuts." Now that's passion. When you express a desire, you have a better chance of exciting your partner.

Screaming

Screaming can lead to a neighborhood watch on your house or your landlord's desire to evict you. (The standard lease should have a clause "Screaming permitted only during orgasm.")

If you don't make sounds during orgasm, you are depriving both yourself and your partner.

The next time you go to the zoo, take a tape recorder and capture some animal sounds. No, don't tape the cows—we don't want any moos during orgasm. Tape the monkeys and play this tape during lovemaking. Our ancestors will inspire you.

Comments: Words and sounds are important during lovemaking. If you hold back language, you may also hold back physical release. Words and sounds also create an atmosphere of approval. Don't hold back; let go of any sound that reflects your joy.

Fantasy

It is no big deal to have fantasies, because everyone has fantasies. It is a big deal to have the courage to share your fantasies. If you begin to share your fantasies, your partner will be encouraged to do the same.

You may be walking down the street with your partner and be aroused because of a travel agency sign:

FOR ONLY $69
FALL DOWN TO VIRGINIA

All of a sudden you are aroused with passion. Say to your partner, "That sign makes me want to fall on you." Your partner will be flattered that you were aroused, and more important, your partner will be impressed that you shared your fantasy.

You may have fantasies about changing the location of your lovemaking. You may want to try it on top of the kitchen table, under the living room skylight, or on the front lawn of your parents' house. After you share your fantasies, it is OK to go ahead and try them out, but certain ones are better left on the talking level. Don't make love in front of your parents' house, it will lower real estate values.

Comments: *In the fantasy world of the partnership, couples love to give pet names to their private parts. Sharing these names during casual conversation builds a bond of trust. This stimulates sexuality.*

Do not hesitate to use these names, to share fantasies, and to celebrate your physical need for each other. This type of language builds intimacy: "Me take pipi for a walk." "Me see your petunia."

Perhaps you think this type of language is insane, but it really makes all of us feel loved.

Toolbox

Do not be embarrassed to talk about sexual tools to be used during lovemaking. The vibrator, for many, has become an important aid to lovemaking.

Treat your partner to a vibrator and say, "Our lovemaking will be more fun with help from the local public utility company."

If your partner looks embarrassed, just explain, "We go twenty beats per minute, while this thing goes twenty thousand beats per second."

Your partner will understand.

Comments: *The vibrator should be used for fun and not reprisal. I met one wife who was angry about her husband's watching football every weekend. She refused to be a football widow. During the game, she used the vibrator in a nearby room. This caused a vibration on the TV screen. He got furious.*

We worked out a compromise. Halftime became lovemaking time.

Avoid Perversion

Perversion causes pain; depravity, on the other hand, can cause intimacy. Avoid pain by replacing perverse ideas with depraved thoughts.

Perhaps you would like to whip and chain your partner. This perversion obviously could lead to pain. By substituting harmless depravity you get all of the pleasure and none of the pain.

It certainly would be a depraved thought to want to place Jell-O and whipped cream on your partner's stomach in order to enjoy dessert. When your partner objects, you should withdraw your request for whipped cream because this would cause a mess. Learn to bargain. Say to your partner, "No whipped cream, only Jell-O." Your flexibility will bring closeness, and this playfulness will bring tenderness.

If your partner does not object to the whipped cream, you might consider having dessert in the bathtub. It makes doing the "dishes" much easier.

Comments: *I have met couples who use drugs to get a "high" during sex. This so-called "high" really leads to mutual contempt because each partner knows that the other is afraid to open up to intimacy. It is perverse to think that a drug will free you.*

I recommend that couples get a "high" with prune juice. You might feel disgusted by the idea, but as a child I was told that this "will open you up," so, I am sharing this secret with you.

Adultery Without Sex

Sure it is exciting to think about having a relationship outside of marriage. But that doesn't mean you have to act on your thoughts. You can use Primitive Communication instead. If you are approached or are approaching someone else, be mature and say, "My partner likes my pipi" or "My partner likes my petunia."

This statement will shift the focus from genitals to language. This is not seduction. You are stating that sexual feelings can be talked about, but these feelings do not have to be acted on.

Comments: So many people believe that adultery occurs because of a physical need. Wrong. Adultery happens because of an inability to express oneself. If you can't talk to your partner, then you hide this defect by engaging in an outside relationship.

If you know how to use language, then you can repair your basic relationship. If you wish to be involved with others, then you can talk to others, once you know how to talk— but you do not need to be physically involved.

Musical Excitation

Musical rhythms can have an inspirational effect on couples. You and your partner should buy bongos. In the serenity of your hut, slowly tap your bongos and say to each other, "We beat bongos." This rhythmic beat will cause an increased sense of physical awareness, which should culminate in a passionate sensual encounter.

The next morning, when you leave your compound for the daily vocational trek, you will catch the 7:05, and there will be an unusual smile on your face. Your train compartment will be filled with tense, rigid, and hysterical individuals all worried about the latest economic forecast. A stranger will sit next to you and say, "Aren't you concerned about inflation?" You will turn to the stranger and say, "Today I am not worried about interest rates because last night my bongos were banged."

This stranger will disappear from your life forever.

Comments: When speaking to your partner, monitor the way you speak. Your tonality, rhythm, and cadence will create a climate of either warmth or coldness.

If you speak like a Marine drill instructor, you may wind up drilling alone to the numbers 1, 2, 3, 4 and 1, 2, 3, 4. But if you speak in a gentle and loving manner, then you may wind up thrilling with your partner to the numbers 68 + 1, 68 + 1. . . .

TASK MENU

If your partner became too excited over the expansion of your intimacy muscle, then you may have become fearful and experienced a relapse. Don't become frightened; keep practicing Primitive Communication, and the relapse should not last a long time. I mention this because sexuality can be intimidating. I'm going to go easy on you this week because I know it's difficult to express your sexuality verbally. I would be happy if you just did one of the following:

- Said to your partner, "Me available."
- Let out a small scream when making love.
- Complimented your partner's private part.
- Touched your private part and said, "Hello, old friend."

Now I know that the last task is easy. I gave you the option because I wanted you to be successful. Do you get a special treat for this? Of course you do.

Special Treat Become the Primate of the Month. Draw a nude picture of yourself and give it to your partner. Don't forget to autograph it.

Topic 5: Family

A family is really an extended partnership. You may have many partners—spouse, child, grandparent, and in-law. These relationships should be supportive, but many times they become disasters. Family relationships should nurture you, not cause malnutrition.

While Primitive Language (Me for I, grunts and groans, odd vocabulary choices, bad grammar) should be kept between you and your partner, other principles of PC will help to bring your family closer. For example, it would be good to follow the PC tactic of talking to your child while touching her, but instead of saying, "Me touch," say, "I love you." You can do this with your parents and siblings, too. Try some family tactics in order to learn how to use your family to build security in your life.

Ideas: The Family and Power
Parenting
The Family Network

Tactics: A Tribe of Two
Tribal Meetings
Holidays
Parental Rights
Feuding over Junior
Junior Becomes Enlightened
Junior Learns to Fly
Junior Falls in Love
When Junior Comes Marching Home
New Hunting Grounds

Task Menu

IDEAS

The Family and Power

Here is a typical picture of a family: everyone is sitting around the dining room table, eating turkey, and talking about the planned picnic. Is this reality? Perhaps, but it may resemble more closely some type of science fiction. The typical family more closely resembles the science of friction.

A family goes through various cycles of being close and distant. It is no picnic going through these cycles. A family is usually in flux because each member has different ideas and needs, which results in multiple levels of power within the family structure. When power is distributed unevenly, reactions take many forms, including depression, anger, withdrawal, suicide, and stress.

Primitive Communication helps to redistribute power within a family. With Primitive Communication, those with power signal that they are willing to reduce this power, and those members who are powerless obtain a better sense of their own strength. With this rebalancing, friction is reduced. Primitive Communication acts as a lubricant.

Parenting

Parents have a fantasy that they train their children. I hate to report this, but a child starts at birth to train you. For example, if the child cries, you pick it up. It is important for partners to have a strong alliance in order to survive this training program.

Do not try to help each other with theories of child psychology. Do not say to your partner, "If we would pay more attention and buy more toys, then Junior would be satisfied and feel loved." This type of language will drive you both nuts. Be honest and loving and say to each other, "Help." Once this feeling of helplessness is shared, you will stop pretending that you feel comfortable with Junior's training program, which is inflicted on both of you.

If you are alone in raising a child (parent without partner), it is important to have some type of support network. With the right type of support by either a partner or others, you can disengage from your child's needs enough to continue to shape your own identity.

One day you will solo and receive your engraved wings with the inscription "Parent Without Palpitations."

The Family Network

A family should contain a network of people who are supportive of one another. Each member has certain strengths that at times allow other members to be weak. These strengths lead to mutual support. The motto "in sickness and in health" reflects the sense of unity and confidence each member should feel.

In reality, too many families resemble animal shelters—each member is chained and barking, waiting to be fed. Each member feels alone and frightened.

It is not difficult for family members to reach out to each other by using the principles of Primitive Communication. This moves the family toward health and healing, toward tribal trust.

TACTICS

A Tribe of Two

Do not feel guilty if you stay as a family of two. By choice or other reasons, you may not want (or be able) to expand your tribe. Say to your partner, "We two make family together. Together we whole. We hold each other forever."

Tribal Meetings

Don't meet your partner (and children) informally. Call for a formal tribal meeting. The call to a meeting ends feelings of aloneness and can be an effective part of both psychological and physical healing. It's great to feel that you are part of a team.

Call for a meeting by banging on a kitchen pot. Before sitting down to chat, all in the tribe should hold hands and say something nice. Perhaps you could take turns choosing the "motto of the week."

Comments: *Families need to create a mechanism to give and get feedback. When feelings are not shared, judgmental manipulations build up. A family, a tribe, should gather to share feelings—it's good medicine.*

Being silly together sets the stage for honest sharing. This strengthens a family. Anxieties are revealed, independence is asserted, risks are taken, boundaries are clarified, and more trust develops.

Now that's the way to run a family. Do this and you'll discover that some of your problems have obvious solutions that were previously hidden.

Holidays

Partners get exhausted from holidays. There is pressure from buying gifts and from visiting relatives. Avoid this trap. Tell your partner, "Me take holiday from holiday."

Plan a day free from anxiety, a day without pressure. Make up a holiday card to celebrate this day and give the card to your partner. It should state, "Happy Nothing Day."

Your partner will be delighted with this card because there will be no pressure to give you a gift in return.

Comments: *I have seen too many partners who go to war at holiday time. Many of the pressures revolve around family responsibilities. These so-called responsibilities involve territorial warfare: "We visited your mother, and now we have to visit my mother." When this air-raid alarm is sounded, each partner feels like a prisoner of war.*

It is important to escape from this trap by reducing expectations. Plan holidays without responsibility.

Parental Rights

As Junior grows up, he or she will begin to set boundaries on your rights. At times you will be molested and beaten into submission. During this contest of wills, you will need to articulate your rights and fight for your survival.

Let's say Junior is into biting or pinching. Do not say, "Why are you biting my arm?" Also do not bite Junior back. By doing these things you show Junior you are in a power struggle with him. Instead, assert your parental rights. Unhook from the power struggle. Look at your arm and say, "That hurts. I'm going to go to my room and read to make myself feel better," or "I need a spoonful of ice cream to make myself feel better." Don't give any to Junior. You are signaling that you are taking care of yourself, you are not a target, and you won't be pulled into Junior's manipulations. Junior will probably never bite you again.

Comments: *I had a tough time pulling one couple away from Junior's training schedule. Mom thought a submissive approach would appease Junior, and Dad thought a tough approach was needed, although Dad was too "busy" at work to get involved. So when Mom and Dad were talking in the evening, Junior would throw temper tantrums—pretty smart for an eight-year-old.*

I told the two exhausted parents to get off Junior's training program. When he went into his tantrum, they were to twirl banana skins over their heads and make monkey sounds.

Poor Junior. He stopped his tantrums because he thought that his parents were acting weird.

Feuding over Junior

So many times when partners feud over Junior, they are really fighting each other. Junior should not be brought into the argument when the issue is between partners.

If you are angry at your partner, do not say, "You idiot, you are spoiling Junior." This statement will keep Junior in the fight, and you may not get to the real issue between you and your partner.

Instead, say, "Me upset; me need to talk." There is no attack, and Junior is out of the picture. If you do have a real issue over Junior, then your partner will listen. This will strengthen your bond and keep you both out of Junior's bondage.

Comments: *Junior can sense his parents need an issue in order to avoid looking at their relationship and will usually collude by acting up and providing an issue.*

I worked with one couple who kept going to the brink of divorce. They feuded with each other over the proper method of raising Junior. The father was tough, and the mother was permissive. They threatened each other with divorce, and they avoided talking about their dissatisfaction with each other. When Junior sensed that the divorce issue might be real, he was able to drown it out by getting into bed-wetting. The parents then focused on Junior's problems and stopped talking about a divorce.

I told the parents to stop feuding over Junior and to start confronting each other. I asked them to set aside "confrontation time" each evening. I even asked them to say, "Me tell you about my needs. Me need to be heard." They learned to listen to each other.

By using Primitive Communication the parents were able to deal directly with each other, and they stopped turning Junior into an invalid.

Junior Becomes Enlightened

Somewhere between the ages of twelve and eighteen. Junior may become enlightened. When this happens, Junior's hair becomes a mohawk, enhanced with pink dye, his nose displays seventeen earrings, and Junior wears combat boots. If you see this change, do not become worried—become bizarre.

Junior will come home and say, "I am breaking out of the chains of this moronic, mundane, middle-class, elitist society." This is enlightenment.

Do not say, "Why are you doing this to me?" Instead, raise your fist and say, "Free the Indianapolis 500."

Junior will think that you have also become enlightened.

Comments: *Parents go insane during these years of enlightenment. You will waste your time trying to reason with Junior.*

One of the best ways of saving yourself is to be illogical. Junior finds you too predictable. If you can be unpredictable, you will save yourself, because then Junior will be less likely to molest you. But if you keep trying to use logic and reason with Junior, then you'll be tested even more.

I am not saying that you should approve of Junior's attitudes and behaviors; I just don't want you to become a slave to Junior's rebellion. You've given him all the tools to become a healthy person. If you refuse to rise to his challenge, he'll get bored, and pretty soon he'll look for other things to do—like open his toolbox.

Junior Learns to Fly

When Junior is fifteen, he or she will come home and tell you that kids at school are using drugs. You will feel safe because Junior is confiding in you. This relieves you of the idea that Junior is flying with the other kids.

Do not be deceived. Junior may be a test pilot or even a flying ace. You or your partner should say, "I'm going on alert—I don't want you to be a space cadet." Junior now knows that you will be watching to see if she or he qualifies as a space cadet.

Very quietly, put on your warrior's outfit and become active in the community.

Comments: Do not look the other way because other kids are using drugs. If all the parents look away, then who is minding the store? Junior gave you a warning about what is going on—listen to this warning.

As you become more active, Junior will see that you mean business. Junior will be less likely to try to fool an active parent. If Junior is a drug user, have the courage to shoot his spacecraft out of the sky. Go for it.

Junior Falls in Love

When Junior is sixteen, she will come home and announce that she is in love. You will be told that this is the real thing.

After you are revived, you will start to cross-examine her: "Is he from a good family?" "Does he want to go to medical school?" "What's his religion?"

If you do this, you are in for trouble.

Say to Junior, "We need to learn about your partner."

Junior will be surprised and pleased by this response. After all, you passed the big test. You listened to Junior, and she knows she has a friend at home.

Comments: As a child ages, families are tested. As a parent, you do not have to accept your child's behavior, but you must listen to Junior.

If you do not listen to feelings, then your child will be angry and more likely to rebel. When you listen, your child will feel less of a need to test you.

When Junior Comes Marching Home

Partners sometimes get paralyzed when Junior returns home after graduation from college. You have lost your zest for loud music and do not wish to be awakened at night to talk about Plato.

To survive, use Primitive Communication. When Junior walks through the door with a diploma, before she can say anything, say: "We do not want an academic inquisition."

When Junior hears this, expect to be referred for therapy. But unless you set up boundaries right away, you are in trouble. If so, pack your bags and go on a ten-year safari.

Comments: *I have seen so many partners become invalids when their kid moves back home after college.*

I worked with a couple who told me that they became anxious upon the return of the great scholar. I told them that anxiety was an understatement. I told them that they were hysterical. The week that Junior returned, they both began to lose their hair. It's enough that they lost their shirt because of the tuition loans, but it was too much to lose their scalps.

Parents usually feel too guilty to admit they no longer want their grown children to live at home. I told this couple not to feel guilty, to look at each other and say, "Me no want to live with Junior no more." Only when they admitted this to each other were they able to help Junior find a place of his own.

New Hunting Grounds

There may come a time when you want a new partner and you feel that only a new hunting ground will provide you with your needs. Try Primitive Communication before you move on. Even if the partnership is over, Primitive Communication can still aid in this shift. It is especially important when little apes are involved.

Both of you want the best for your little ones. They will feel better if you try to reach your partner than if you attempt to go for your partner's head and hang it over the fireplace mantel.

In front of the little ones, don't say, "You idiot." Rather, say, "We didn't make it, but look at the beautiful monkey we produced."

If you do not do this, your beautiful monkey could turn into a gorilla.

Comments: *Too many people get divorced and continue the power struggle through the children. Even if you are divorcing, you should use Primitive Communication. You will both be parents forever, and even longer than that. If you can bring about an armistice in issues involving the children, then you can make decisions that are truly in the best interests of the child. Do not involve a child in combat.*

If you call this truce and begin to combat your need to inflict pain, your child will survive the divorce. A truce can lead to that beautiful moment in life when your child graduates from college, looks at both of you, and says, "Mom and Dad, you couldn't live together, but at least together you have let me live—by the way, I forgot to pay the car insurance."

TASK MENU

You are probably beginning to dream about getting a trophy or diploma for building intimacy skills. You *will* be rewarded, but for now, keep building your skills.

I expect a lot from you this week—you should have done all of these activities:

- Called a tribal meeting
- Stopped catering to the child in your house, perhaps by telling Junior, "You are talking to an important person."
- Told your partner what was really bothering you instead of pretending it's the kids.
- Listened to your child.

My special treat for you is a special trip.

Special Treat Stop fantasizing about all of those international vacations with the family. Let's get moving. Get everyone to pack their bags, get their passports, and head for the nearest international airport.

On your way to the airport, decide where to go. France? Italy? Japan? Upon your arrival at the airport, watch the planes take off for your favorite country. Then get on line to purchase tickets. When you hear the price of a ticket, get out of the line and head for home. As you leave the airport, look around and say, "Wow, it's great to be home."

Topic 6: Finance

Partners need to use money to improve their inner lives and not to acquire more consumer goods. Improvement may mean having fewer material goods but having more good times. With Primitive Communication tactics, partners will be stimulated to reach for each other, rather than reaching for more acquisitions.

Ideas:	Measuring Success
	Credentials vs. Competency
	From Young Urban Professional to Young Ultraprimate
	Going Prenup
Tactics:	Bonds
	Oatmeal Economics
	Backpack
	Intimacy Credit
	Vacations
	Dining vs. Feeding
	Your Cave
	Cold Calls
	Primitive Elegance
	Freedom from Responsibility

Task Menu

IDEAS

Measuring Success

Success should be judged by our feelings of closeness to our partner. If we play more and enjoy being together, we don't need all of the consumer goods to "fill that void" in our life.

Unfortunately, partners usually measure success by how much they have acquired. We can too easily adapt to an unsuccessful relationship by living in a big house with a pool. If we spent less time acquiring consumer goods, perhaps we would be willing to invest more time in acquiring emotional closeness without a pool.

How many times have our fantasies misled us into thinking that if we just had one more item we would be happy? So we go out and get this item, only to find that we need yet another item. The treadmill is relentless.

If you do use money as a barrier to your partnership, then you might wind up alone, repeating that sacred material mantra: S-H-O-P-P-I-N-G.

Emotional success really depends on emotional closeness. Measure it only by how good you feel.

Credentials vs. Competency

At different times, credentials have been based on ownership, height, class, strength, and gender. During wartime, if a soldier had stepped on a land mine, his buddies, concerned about his future ability to reproduce, would ask about his "credentials."

Currently, money can buy credentials or financial security, but can it buy emotional security? In the high-tech society we live in, great emphasis is given to credentials, sometimes at the expense of emotional competency.

A husband might say to his wife, "You can't control me with a degree in animal husbandry." She might say, "Your law degree will not protect you from alimony." Thus, they may have tried to intimidate each other with credentials rather than supporting each other with emotional competency.

The only real credential that shows that we are emotionally competent is the ability to make each other feel wanted and make ourselves vulnerable. This courage deserves the Medal of Honor. Without this courage, the couple can earn only the Purple Heart.

**From Young Urban Professional
to Young Ultraprimate**

Item	*Young Urban Professional*	*Young Ultraprimate*
Transportation	BMW	Bicycle
Drink	An understated wine	Banana malted
Portage	Leather luggage	Paper shopping bag
Casual clothes	Designer sweats	Pajamas with feet
Footwear	Reeboks	Sandals
Relaxer	Valium	Prune juice
Hangout	Health club	Zoo
Exercise	Aerobics	Tree swinging

Going Prenup

Often prenuptial agreements are seen as acts of hostility or distrust. A prenup should create trust rather than distrust. If you are interested in the idea, do not hesitate, but make it fun. Suggest drawing up a primitive prenup by saying, "We list our holdings, but we hold each other forever."

Draw up lists and learn more about each other.

Comments: *So many couples have money problems even before a marriage. I worked with one engaged couple who were so hysterical that they were unable to make an appointment with an attorney. They wanted a prenuptial agreement.*

I told them that they had to draw up a primitive prenup in order to learn about each other. I gave them crayons and construction paper, and they wrote:

I keep my crayons.
I keep my computerized abacus.
We share our sandbox.
If we have two little apes, then the screamer goes to camp at age six months, and we both share the costs.

This fun primitive prenup reduced their anxiety and fears, and they were able to make an appointment to see an attorney.

TACTICS

Bonds

When we shop for a mate, we look for lots of different things: charm, sense of humor, warmth, ability to earn big bucks. Which of these doesn't quite fit here?

It's important that we look at each other as people, not as commodities. Say to your partner, "Me love you even if you become ditch digger." If your partner is a ditch digger, say, "Me love you even if you become bank president."

This kind of acceptance gives your partner emotional security that makes financial security seem much less crucial. Emotional bonds are always worth more than savings bonds.

Oatmeal Economics

Couples can easily develop a passion for spending and an aversion to saving. It is important to first develop the habit of saving instead of focusing on the amount.

Place an empty oatmeal box or coffee can in the middle of your kitchen table and label this jar "Freedom Fund" or "Wampum."

Before each morning feeding, place a few coins in the jar and say to your partner: "For me and you."

Comments: *Money is a medium of exchange, and we need it. Smart apes save money ("for a rainy day" or to send Junior to college) not to hoard it or to buy unnecessary luxuries, but to buy freedom from worry. Saving money together is a good way to remind yourselves of the fun times that lie ahead and to ensure that nothing will get in the way of the fun. Especially thrifty apes spend their later years taking great trips, such as African safaris, or buying great condos in tropical climes like Florida and California. Ape heaven.*

Backpack

If you feel burdened by possessions, try this fantasy: imagine that all your worldly possessions fit into a backpack. Once you've visualized what it is you really need, actually try to get rid of some of the things you don't need. The goal is freedom from clutter. Then go out and buy a backpack and say to your partner, "No more junk. If no fits in pack, me no want."

Comments: The next time you feel lured by an advertisement, like "For only $12,000, buy your own planet, only 10 percent down," remember your backpack. Fight this urge to acquire. Do not buy a planet. Go the way of the jungle. Buy a banana for 30¢. Put the $11,999.70 in the bank.

Intimacy Credit

We've all been trained to live on credit. It is so easy to get out the old credit card and charge away. Fly now, pay later.

Instead of running up big bills, try building up intimacy credit. Do something now that gets you a reward later. Don't pay bills; pay attention to your partner. The attention can be in the form of inexpensive, silly, witty, loving forms of giving. Do it and your credit rating will zoom.

Give your partner a primitive gift for no reason—a basket of fruit, a bag of fresh noodles, a ball of twine, a necklace of paper clips, or a back massage. As you give the gift, say, "Me credit my account with love." You have built intimacy credit and reduced your financial liabilities at the same time.

Vacations

So you and your partner want to charge a luxurious vacation on your credit card and tell all of your friends about this vacation.

Don't do it. Instead, take a vacation from spending money.

Take a few days off and go to a public park or library or tell your partner, "We go zoo." Wear your best jungle outfit, eat peanuts, be selfish (do not share the peanuts with the animals), and don't tell your friends about your wonderful vacation.

Comments: *Don't delay trying this, because you'll miss out on a lot of fun. Isn't it great to think you can have a vacation whenever you want it?*

Dining vs. Feeding

A vacation from food preparation usually means dining out. It is so expensive to "dine" that many people will even forgo dating just to save money. If you regularly spend $50 to go out to eat, it is now time to engage in primitive dining.

It's OK to go out to eat without making a major event of it. I want you to take your partner out for a simple dinner. Say, "We go feeding." Go to your local coffee shop and order one of the following:

- Bananas and sour cream
- Bananas and pot cheese
- Bananas and ice cream
- Bananas and blueberries
- Burger and fries

As you can see, there is a wide variety of foods that can be ordered, and the evening will cost about $9. Be sure to talk to your "date" about something other than food.

Then come home and settle down for a quiet evening with a tasty drink. I recommend pineapple juice.

With this new feeding pattern you can both now concentrate on the relationship and take a vacation from debt.

Your Cave

We have trained ourselves to need expansive living space. As builders shift from one-family houses to multifamily units, and housing costs escalate, we feel deprived because we cannot get our dream space.

It's not bad to think small. With a large space, we may have room and privacy, and we can create separate functions, such as "cooking in my kitchen" or "reading in my den." But this privacy may also lead couples to function in isolation.

To combat this, fantasize that your house or co-op is a cave. Get a double sleeping bag, say to your partner, "We sleep well in small spaces," and experiment with sleeping in different spaces where you live. You'll also sleep better with a smaller mortgage.

Comments: *So many of our spending habits render us invalids. I worked with one couple who were compulsive home buyers and decorators. As soon as they bought and decorated, they would need to move. They did not make a profit in these moves. These partners were engaged in a massive power struggle. Because they could not manage to redecorate their relationship, they avoided each other by doing busywork.*

I asked them to pitch a tent in their living room, sleep in a sleeping bag, place sand around their tent, and place my picture inside the tent.

After a few days of cursing my picture, they began to laugh and talk in primitive and affectionate ways. I knew they had begun to redecorate their relationship when they threw away my picture.

Cold Calls

Your hut is invaded by a call from a stockbroker. This usually happens during lovemaking. Do not be rude—the broker is only trying to make a living. The broker will say, "Would you like us to examine your portfolio? Our new asset allocation program is intended to help you meet your goals."

You then say, "Me buy rubber trees. Me corner the market in condoms."

This broker will not call you again.

Comments: *So many partners complain to me that telephone intruders interfere with their privacy. Use Primitive Communications to fend off the invaders.*

Primitive Elegance

Partners can get into trouble with fantasies of elegant living. Trying to be an elitist, above the crowd, can put unbearable pressure on a relationship. Elegance as a goal has its price both financially and emotionally. Your partnership may suffer from publicity at the expense of privacy.

This fantasy can cause a couple to buy a charming country barn that is immediately equipped with the latest high-tech sound system and outdoor hot tub. This country barn will go on display to relatives and friends.

To be really sophisticated, you must reach down to primitive goals that do not require an audience of friends or relatives. Privacy is more important than publicity.

Keep your barn simple. If your guest bed sags, just tell your friends it's because the cows sleep there. Your friends won't want to stay overnight. You and your partner will be privy to a privacy that only primates enjoy. You will also not be visited by in-laws.

Comments: *Fancy living may give you convenience, but it does not necessarily bring you closeness. Do not let high style or technology dominate your lives. The simplicity of primitive living can lead to fun and intimacy. You learn to protect each other rather than relying on a showpiece to protect you.*

Freedom from Responsibility

It is too easy to dream of freedom from responsibility without ever doing anything about it. If you feel that the burdens of cleaning, shopping, and paying bills dominate your relationship, then it's time for a break from burdens. Say to your partner, "Time out from responsibility."

Take a few hours off. Sit on the floor of the house and relax. Offer your partner a banana. Chant, "Never put a banana in the refrigerator." Do somersaults. Tell dirty jokes.

Take turns suggesting this time-out. Freedom from responsibility can occur if you are both willing to be silly.

If you do not take this kind of time-out, then you and your partner will both feel the weight of these burdens. With silliness the weight of the burdens is shared.

TASK MENU

By now, I suspect your friends are starting to become jealous of your intimacy skills. You have been exercising, and now it is starting to pay off. This week, I hope that you did at least two of the following:

- Began a small savings program.
- Donated some possessions to a thrift shop.
- Planned an inexpensive vacation.
- Ate at an inexpensive restaurant.
- Shared some dreams of reducing responsibility.

These ideas may sound simple, but for many they are a major reversal in the way they live. I know it was a struggle for you to reverse binging on consumerism, but now you have a reward coming.

Special Treat Look through your living quarters and find something you do not need. Sell this item. It can be a stamp, picture, coat, rug, ring, camera, or anything else. You do not have a need for this item.

What are you going to do with the money? I want you to buy an expensive item. Go out and buy a high-priced piggy bank to replace your oatmeal box.

Congratulations. You have just become a serious saver.

Topic 7: Maturation

With maturity, we should become more skilled in reaching our partner. Unfortunately, maturation can often mean a rigidity that is set in concrete. Learning flexibility, a lifelong process, is the real test of maturity.

Ideas: Longevity
Romantic Pattern-Making
Premature "Senility"
From Nursery to Nursing Home

Tactics: Retirement
Heirlooms
Wrinkles
Codes
Illness
Vintage Romance
Grooming and Groping

Task Menu

IDEAS

Longevity

Longevity in a partnership does not necessarily mean peaceful coexistence. Some long-term relationships are in reality contracts for long-term suffering. Each partner feels cannibalized—eaten alive—and never manages to escape this pain through a healthy divorce. Instead, partners forever maintain their mutual pain alliance.

Couples are not heroic by staying together if they are eating each other alive. It is heroic, however, to begin to learn about intimacy no matter how long you have been ineffective with each other. It is true that you are never too old to learn.

You may feel that you have tried everything and nothing worked. I do not believe that you have tried everything until you have tried Primitive Communication.

Primitive Communication defeats the longevity excuse ("We can't change; we have been married for thirty years"). Primitive Communication gives you a fresh start because it is a new way of talking. The difficulties of the past are put aside, and your relationship is renewed.

Romantic Pattern-Making

After the coupling process begins, partners often try to engage in romantic redesigning. Before commitment, most couples think they have a pretty good idea of how the partner will fit in. After the commitment, however, many people find the fit too loose or too tight and begin to design a new pattern. Their new designs may clash with their partner's fashion ideas. The battle has now begun. Each partner tries to squeeze the other into a garment made out of antique patterns. "It fits others, so why not you?"

Maturity occurs when you begin to adapt your design to the actual configuration of your partner, not the imaginary outline that stimulated the new design.

Premature "Senility"

It's too bad that young couples don't enjoy the benefits of senility. If young partners do not answer the telephone, write while on vacation, turn off the lights, or they make noise while kissing, they are accused of being selfish. If an elderly couple behaves this way, people excuse them by saying, "Well, it's their age."

Rules of proper behavior can lead to distance between partners of all ages. Make a pact with your partner to engage in some "senile" and primitive acts: bathe each other; occasionally forget to call the relatives; make noises while kissing in public. When eating soup in a restaurant, be sure to drip some on your lap. Be sloppy and silly. Say to each other, "We old. We enjoy each other."

Senile behavior will bring closeness because you have made an important alliance, a pact against conventional behavior. Don't worry if people begin to avoid you; it is not because you are antisocial. It is because you smell like mushroom and barley soup.

From Nursery to Nursing Home

All of us are in a state of transition from nursery to nursing home. During this transition you will build up a set of experiences with some very important people in your life.

Your early experiences will be with a parent or parents. In most cases, you will be nurtured and made to feel secure. At some point you will shift to a special partner. You will then build up a set of experiences with this partner. You may even expand your tribe by having little apes.

To face aging without this tribe can make your later years a lonely experience. But with Primitive Communication your experience will not be lonely. You have learned to be there for your tribe, and your tribe will want to be there for you. With this tribe, your later years can be a lovely experience.

At last, when you are wheeled into a nursing home, with the joy of having been close to your tribe, and having known what it is to be important to someone else, you will know that it was all worthwhile. At this point in your life, you may not know the time of day, but you'll at least have had the time of your life.

TACTICS

Retirement

Retirement planning should start on the first day of your partnership. Partners do not realize that it is too late to face retirement at retirement. When you know your options, you are liberated from worrying about your future.

Signal your interest to your partner by saying, "We plan our retirement." Let the following suggestions inspire you:

1. Open IRAs together.
2. Buy nursing home insurance.
3. Start a piggy bank fund earmarked for false teeth.
4. Stockpile blank photo albums for pictures of grandchildren.

Without this planning, you run the risk of becoming a prisoner of your retirement. When this occurs, you are not headed for liberation: you are headed for solitary confinement.

Comments: *Go bozo over your retirement fantasies. Nothing is too weird. Share everything with your partner. As you do this you'll develop new ideas and discover new things about yourself and your partner.*

135

Heirlooms

It is important for partners to create heirlooms together. These heirlooms should be fun toys that partners play with, come to love, and only incidentally pass down to their (bewildered) children. Normally, adult toys are cars and sailboats. But these toys should be of value only for what they symbolize to a couple.

Future heirlooms might be:

- A walking staff
- That special nightie
- A sled
- Nude pictures of each other
- A ship model
- Primitive statuary
- A canoe paddle

The world will not know about your secret toy symbols, but these sacred symbols will remind you both of the strength and beauty of your love. As the toys age and your journey gets shorter, your toys will serve as a reminder of your passionate embraces, when you each asked, "Can I paddle your canoe, oar something else?"

Comments: If your heirlooms have great monetary value, your successors will fight over them; this is not a good legacy. Better to leave them confused.

Wrinkles

If partners are lucky, they will age together. Many partners are proud of their longevity, but many try to hide their wrinkles. With the cosmetic approach, wrinkles are hidden with dyes, "erased" by chemicals, or even removed through surgery.

Too much money and time is spent on hiding wrinkles, and more time should be spent on making your partner feel attractive. Stroke your partner's face and say, "Me love your baby skin."

With tenderness, we can smooth out our partner's feelings about aging. This will iron out many wrinkles.

Comments: *Primitive Communication is also a wonderful technique to use on aging parents. Take an aging parent in your arms and say, "My Mama, my Papa, me give huggy-poo." Your parent will smile and forgive you for all the aggravation you caused when you were growing up.*

Codes

After you have been partners awhile, the Intimacy Dictionary (your personal ID) is no longer necessary. You will find you have actually developed your own code. Code words and gestures will release a torrent of good feelings within your partner that will add ease and pleasure to your relationship. For example, when you say to your partner, "Darling, we putter around garden," he or she understands you perfectly. Ecstasy follows when your partner overpowers you with a loving response: "Our roots are strong."

Comments: As a relationship ripens, partners develop all sorts of codes. In time these often go beyond words. A certain glance, sigh, or touch may come to mean something just to the two of you. These codes are special to the relationship.

Illness

Of course you need your partner
more when you are ill. At this
time, it is important to show
gratitude and appreciation. Do
not hide your dependency on
your partner when you are ill,
because this makes your partner
feel unloved.

To act dependent when you
are ill is an important part of
the nurturing process. Say to
your partner, "My fever gives me
hots for you." Your partner will
say, "You are delirious, so drink
water and get the fever down."
Secretly, your partner will feel
loved and wanted because you
are showing your needs.

Do not say to your partner, "I
caught this cold from you when
you opened the window." This
form of communication will give
your partner a cold chill, too. Do
not hide your dependency by
accusing your partner. Say to
your partner, "Me need you—we
partners."

Your partner will feel your
dependency and your needs.
Your message will be easy to
decode, and you will not be
alone in fighting your illness.

Vintage Romance

Like a good wine, a romance should get better with age. Stop thinking it is for the young; it is for all ages.

Go to your partner and say, "Me age like wine. Me taste better now."

Your partner may think that you have lost your marbles, but after you open your vat, your partner will love the taste and give up alcohol.

Grooming and Groping

As partners age, there seems to be an emphasis on grooming but not enough emphasis on groping. Touching each other will help you both look good. You'll look well groomed. Say to your partner, "Me groom you and me grope your best part."

Is this a way for adults to talk? You bet it is. Your partner will be ecstatic hearing this even on your sixty-ninth wedding anniversary.

Comments: *Partners should not feel that touching is just for the young. If you touch each other, then you both stay young. This is the Fountain of Youth.*

141

TASK MENU

Any good exercise program requires a time-out. You can rest your intimacy muscle and take pride in your accomplishments. In fact, I think I'll list only one task that I hope you've done this week:

• You both took care of each other.

Do you get a special treat for this accomplishment? Of course you do.

Special Treat People seem to love tests—once they're out of school. So here's a fun one to determine your level of competency with Primitive Communication. Enjoy it.

Self-Mastery Test

Are you afraid you haven't progressed enough in your relationship? See how much you've learned by taking this short test.

Choose one answer. At the end of the test you will find the correct answers.

1. "Why don't you tell me that you love me?" means:
   a. Where are your brains?
   b. Stop acting dumb.
   c. Are you still in love with your mother?
   d. Me need you.
2. "You stopped giving me gifts" means:
   a. Lend me your credit card.
   b. I need an annuity.
   c. You need new medication.
   d. Me need to be noticed.
3. "I know that you have sexual problems" means:
   a. Don't touch me.
   b. Stop looking in the mirror.
   c. Why can't you act out your fantasies?
   d. Me need to be touched.
4. "You don't listen to me" means:
   a. You need a hearing aid.
   b. Please turn off the TV set.
   c. You are quiet because you are angry.
   d. Me need to feel close.
5. "Are you really interested in me?" means:
   a. Are you seeing others?
   b. Will you abandon me?
   c. Forget about old romances.
   d. Me want you.
6. "Why can't you be affectionate?" means:
   a. You are a cold person.

b. You don't care for me.

c. Why are you afraid of intimacy?

d. Me need hug.

7. "Why did you flirt with that cashier?" means:

    a. You are in debt to me.

    b. You have no credit with me.

    c. Aren't you too old to flirt?

    d. Me insecure.

8. "Our relationship lacks passion" means:

    a. You need a sex therapist.

    b. Why is food so important to you?

    c. You have psychological problems.

    d. Me need to feel wanted.

9. "Why do you have to talk to the waiter—can't we just order?" means:

    a. You talk too much.

    b. You are too ambivalent.

    c. Let us not have another fight.

    d. Me hungry.

ANSWERS

If you chose *d* as the answer to each question, you are correct. You are now competent in Primitive Communication, and I congratulate you. Your diploma is on the next page. You earned it. The diploma should be presented at a dignified academic ceremony. Appropriate academic costume would be pajamas. The graduation music should be chosen by the organ player.

If you missed any answer, you may still be thinking too much and not experiencing enough. As an intellect junkie, you probably need to read the next section, "Remedial Insight." You have a passionate need for ideas that can help you redirect your thinking. That's okay—for now. However, once you've read "Remedial Insight," be sure to go back to basics.

The Professors and Zookeepers of
THE UNIVERSITY OF INTIMACY
confer upon

_____

the degree of
MASTER OF BANANA

Date _____

SEAL:

signed by duly authorized officers

_____

President

_____

Zookeeper

Note: To make official, sign your name, date, and fill in seal with red crayon.

The Professors and Zookeepers of
THE UNIVERSITY OF INTIMACY
confer upon

_____

the degree of
MASTER OF BANANA

Date _____

SEAL:

signed by duly authorized officers

_____

President

_____

Zookeeper

Note: To make official, sign your name, date, and fill in seal with red crayon.

WARNING
Do Not Read This Section Unless You Are a Hopeless
Intellect Junkie.

Remedial Insight

I know that you are tempted to read this section. If you have followed my advice, it is not necessary to do so. I do know, however, that even with a better relationship, you may still want to know "why." Just be careful not to let this section interfere with your improvement. As you read it, forget it.

If you have not followed my directions, then you probably feel a need for remedial insight. Do not let any insights gained from reading this prevent you from using the tactics. You must clear your mind of intellectual clutter to get close to your partner.

Since the whole point of my method involves a return to Primitive Communication, it seems counterproductive to give you my theories about couples issues. Theories involving complex thought and high-level thinking are just what I want to teach you to avoid. Still, I know some of you will not try my techniques without first filling your head with *why* it works. Because my main concern is to help you improve your relationship, I'd rather have you understand a little theory than discount my method before even trying it. But I've placed it in the back of the book in the hope that you will have at least tried some of the tactics before tackling the whys.

A successful relationship is one of life's greatest treasures, yet it is apparently one of the most difficult things to achieve. When couples arrive at my office, they bring with them a multitude of complaints about each other. Each partner believes that if he or she could only get the other to change his or her ways, then everything would be OK.

"If we had sex more often, this relationship would be fine."

"If you would only listen when I tell you something, I wouldn't get so angry at you."

"If you didn't have a problem getting close, we'd be in great shape." The accusations go on and on.

What couples don't realize is that the specific issues they are at war over are only symptoms of a much deeper and more basic problem: their fear of intimacy.

It may come as a surprise, especially to those of you who have believed until this point that you have wanted intimacy ("It's my partner who is resistant"), that a fear of intimacy is at the root of your problems. But if you look under the surface, which this section will help you do, I think you will find my analysis is correct. For you see, if even one of you stops fearing intimacy, your relationship will change dramatically.

Very often, your relationship problems themselves are created solely for the purpose of avoiding intimacy. If you are embroiled in complex negative dynamics, you never have to face the fear of becoming close. By "close" I do not mean you've had great sex. Nor does closeness necessarily imply knowing every little thing about each other. For unlike more traditional couples theories, my premise is that couples don't need to understand each other, question each other, or know each other's family histories to get close. You need to know only one thing, and that is how to make each other feel safe. It is my belief that if couples do not first experience the possibility of closeness, they may never get through the web of their distancing maneuvers. Even if they are able to understand what they are doing to each other, there is no guarantee the knowledge will lead to intimacy. I say, "Become intimate first. Understand later." Once you feel safe, you are ready for more advanced adventures like understanding, psychological interpretations, emotional insights, and high-level rational thought. If you don't feel safe, these processes are too easily subverted into mechanisms for staying in control and avoiding surrender.

So, when a couple comes to me for therapy, I do not try to unravel their maze of accusations. I go right to the heart of the issue. I teach couples that they can become intimate without in-depth analysis, and I show them how to do it quickly and painlessly. My goal is not understanding, because understanding does not usually work. If it did, couples wouldn't be in therapy for so long (most of my clients stay with me for about six weeks) and people wouldn't buy book after book on love, marriage, and intimacy. My goal is the achievement of intimacy. But the achievement of this goal is not an end in itself: it is the beginning of lifelong growth and sharing.

With this in mind, let's take a closer look at how couples get into trouble and how Primitive Communication helps in its unique way to establish harmony and closeness.

HOW COUPLES GET INTO TROUBLE

Fear of Intimacy

My analysis of how couples get into trouble is a straightforward one. All people long for intimacy and closeness; that's what draws us into a special relationship with a partner in the first place. But each of us is equally afraid of intimacy. To be intimate means to be open and vulnerable to another human being. It means giving up control and allowing ourselves to be known by another.

Often we mistake love or passion for intimacy. The difference is, if we are intimate, love and passion will follow. But feeling love and passion will not necessarily bring us intimacy. The hallmark of intimacy is trust, something much harder to achieve than falling in love. We are not intimate when we meet a stranger and surrender ourselves within minutes. We are teasing ourselves if we call this intimate behavior.

When we are truly intimate, we trust each other and feel safe to express our deepest needs, to say, "I'm scared" or "take care of me," knowing that our partner will not judge us or reject us. We also feel safe to express our joy and strength knowing that our partners will not be jealous or repressive but will be happy with us. This is the gift of intimacy: to know another is with you through your successes and struggles, through your joys and sorrows, and to feel another's failures and triumphs as if they were your own. Intimacy is crying and laughing

153

together, holding each other, encouraging each other, and even argu-ing with each other without trying to destroy the other or fearing you will be destroyed. It is a wonderful experience well worth striving for. Yet most of us fear it as much as we long for it. Why?

Because somewhere along the line we learned that if we are trusting and vulnerable we might get hurt. We could have our heart broken, or we could be controlled or manipulated by another. We fear we may lose our sense of self and drown in the other person, or we fear if we surrender we may be abandoned. In addition, society teaches us through the media that if we are hard and tough, we will succeed. If we are vulnerable, we will be defeated.

The Power Struggle

We avoid what we long for most by creating an elaborate system of self-protection. Though the details of this system may be different in each person, the net result is that we all want to stay in control and keep our partners under control. Of course, if both partners want to be in control, a power struggle must ensue, with each partner trying to keep the other from getting the upper hand; each partner protects himself or herself against possible pain or annihilation. This power struggle is at the heart of every relationship that goes sour. Partners are blind to the fact that they would rather be right than be loved.

Intimidation Tactics

Still, it wouldn't be bad if a couple could face each other and yell, "I'm on top," simultaneously. That would at least be honest and clear communication. Instead, partners develop all kinds of subversive strategies to force each other into submission. I call these strategies *intimidation tactics*. Intimidation can take the form of a direct threat—"If you don't shape up, I'm leaving"—or an underhanded one: "If you get me upset, I'll have a heart attack." The whiner is using intimidation every bit as much as the dictator.

A very common intimidation tactic is the asking of a question. A simple question like "Why were you late?" could be used to intimidate your partner in countless ways. It carries such an expectation that it is the perfect tool for making him or her feel rotten. It could be used to make your partner feel guilty ("The dinner I slaved over is now cold"), to judge him or her ("You're never on time"), or to accuse ("You must have been with someone else"), depending on the tone of voice you use.

In fact, almost anything could be used to intimidate your partner. A partner does not even have to use words when a simple gesture will achieve success. Eyes lifted toward the ceiling in just the right way can be every bit as devastating as a harsh word. Some other obvious tactics include jealousy, physical violence, emotional intensity, becoming ill, sexual demands, withdrawal of sex, threats concerning money or kids, and playing the victim. Then there are less obvious ones, such as giving advice, delivering lectures, and offering psychological interpretations. These are particularly insidious because they come in the guise of help. Even physical affection such as touching and hugging can easily degenerate into just another form of intimidation.

The difficult thing about these interactions is that partners are usually completely unaware of what they are doing. They believe they are justified in their criticisms or their whining, or they believe their questions are only innocent inquiries for information, or they believe they are expressing a feeling. Even when criticisms are justified, they are delivered in a manner that sets up a defensive response.

But the real confusion begins when one partner's intimidation tactics meet the other's. This sets the stage for mass confusion. One partner screams, the other counters by crying. One partner is jealous, the other counters with withdrawal. There are so many permutations that it would take an entire book to go through them all, and that is not the point of my book.

Suffice it to say that by the time couples have spent years intimidating each other, they are so immersed in the battle that they don't even know what they are really fighting about anymore or they are in a quandary as to why their relationship has gone dead. The details of the battle—"She leaves the cap off the toothpaste," "He won't take out the garbage," "She doesn't give me enough sex," "He's jealous of my friends"—become all-important, and the real longing for intimacy stays buried safely under the barrage.

Dependencies

What happens next is partners try to fill the need for intimacy by engaging in what I call *dependent behaviors*. If they are not getting pleasure from their relationship, they attempt to get it in other ways.

155

Smoking, drinking, drugs, overeating, workaholism, materialism, shopping, having affairs, and gambling all become substitutes for the intimacy we lack in our relationship. Even if we don't go this far, dependencies can manifest as less obvious avoidance measures, like watching TV, burying ourselves in books, complaining about our relationships to our friends, inattentiveness, and compulsive talking. Eventually, our dependencies are added to our arsenal of intimidation tactics. We use them to push our partners away. In their extreme, dependencies are the ultimate form of control, because they become the overriding issue in a relationship. There is no room left to do anything else but deal with them. In the end, what was originally sought as a means to pleasure isolates us more and more. The more isolated we become, the more numb we become; the more numb we get, the more frightening it seems to open up to intimacy. Finally, even the thought of letting down with our partner, of becoming vulnerable, is like jumping off a cliff without a hang glider. Who would risk that?

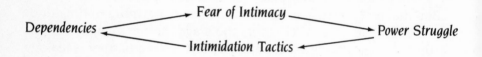

As you can see by the diagram, when couples are in trouble, they really are caught in a vicious circle. It begins with a fear of intimacy. But everything a person or a couple tries to do to assuage this fear only reinforces it, forcing them to repeat the negative cycle over and over again. Primitive Communication breaks this vicious circle by interfering with intimidation tactics, which in turn undercuts the power struggle. When the power struggle is replaced by safety and warmth, the fear of intimacy is reduced. Even dependencies begin to lose their appeal.

When intimidation tactics are replaced by Primitive Communication tactics, intimacy results. When partners have achieved intimacy, they no longer need dependencies to fill up the lonely places or numb their pain. When partners are intimate, they move from dependencies to mutual dependence.

HOW PRIMITIVE COMMUNICATION WORKS
TO BRING ABOUT INTIMACY

The risk of becoming intimate seems enormous when we feel unsafe. What Primitive Communication does is reduce the risk. It gives you the wings of humor, absurdity, warmth, and childlike innocence, made of simple language, simple communication, and simple pleasure. Once you know how to use these wings, you can safely step off that cliff and soar.

If you have gone through my book before reading this, as I hope you have, then you probably by now have some idea of how Primitive Communication accomplishes this goal. What I do is circumvent all the details of a conflict and go directly to the core issue by teaching couples to replace intimidation tactics with Primitive Communication tactics. With a Primitive Communication tactic, couples signal each other that it is safe to be themselves. I help couples create this safe environment by establishing rules that may seem zany or crazy, telling couples exactly what to say to each other or interfering with their high-level reasoning through the use of surprise and absurdity. We have worked so hard to make our relationships complex that it often takes an absurd gesture or word to break the spell and realize that under it all things are really quite simple: "I want to feel safe." "I want to be close." "I need you." Or, to put it in the language of Primitive Communication, "Me need you."

Primitive Communication techniques work even when they are followed in a mechanical way. The gestures or language I provide you with reduce your power to threaten your partner. Your partner in turn feels safer and is less likely to counter with hostility. You then receive a loving response for your efforts. What began as a mechanical exercise has paid off, and you now know Primitive Communication works, so you try it again and again.

Let's look at an example. A wife is very upset by her husband's weight problem. Her usual response would be to eye his protruding belly and lift her eyes to the ceiling. He catches this look and rightly feels she is criticizing him. He responds by asking, "Are you looking at my stomach?" She says, "No." If he's sharp, he'll press on: "Oh yes you were!" Feeling cornered, she'll now launch into the full attack, "OK, I was, but I can't help it, because you're getting as fat as a pig and it

157

turns me off!" Now either he feels helplessly deflated or he screams back, "Lay off me, you bitch!" Both partners end up feeling isolated and angry. All they have to show for this argument is their loneliness.

The same woman, having read *Going Ape*, learns to say to her husband, "Cheeks too chubby," and to lightly pinch his cheeks. At first she does this only because I tell her to try it, but as she utters the words, something softens in her. The words themselves elicit her soft, caring feelings. She has now approached her husband with tenderness instead of hostility, and she has still gotten her point across. He, feeling safe and loved, will now be able to respond nondefensively: "You're right. I've been out of control lately. Will you help me get my diet together?" Husband and wife are now both on the same side, working together for change.

As you can see, this couple never discussed why she had developed a hostile stare or why he felt intimidated by her opinions of him. The simple use of primitive language brought them together. Only now that they are not barking at each other, and have built some trust, are they ready to discuss the tension he's under that caused his weight gain or the fact that her father overate himself into a heart attack. They can hear each other's deepest feelings because they have first established intimacy.

Suppose this husband has a problem with his wife's use of the telephone. She spends hours chatting with her friends. They would end up in a massive power struggle if he said, "Why are your stupid friends so important?" She will retaliate by saying, "You're just too cheap to pay the phone bill!" This is warfare at its best.

By using Primitive Communication, this husband can express himself in a loving way without being judgmental. If he really wants to spend time talking to his wife, I would instruct him to say, "Me miss talking to you." She will not feel judged hearing this statement and will understand that her husband enjoys her company. Because he has not criticized or threatened her, she is free to change her behavior without feeling defensive or angry. She might even apologize.

The Four Basic Primitive Communication Principles

There are four basic Primitive Communication principles:

- Primitive language
- Asking no questions
- Touching and talking
- Humor and absurdity

When one or more of these replaces an intimidation tactic, intimacy is established. Each Primitive Communication principle is designed to create the kind of safety partners need to open up to each other. Though I give specific instructions for each category throughout the book, once you understand the techniques, you are free to create, explore, and experiment. The possibilities are endless.

I have presented primitive language first, because it is the pivotal point of Primitive Communication, but you may find other principles easier to implement. Try them in any order you like.

Primitive Language The most essential principle of Primitive Communication is the use of very basic language when interacting with your partner. We are all so adept at manipulating each other with our sophisticated intellectuality that we have lost the ability to simply connect with each other. With primitive language, you disrupt your normal mode of communication and replace it with a more basic one. You do this in two ways.

1. *Going Ape*

The first task I give to couples who come to me for therapy and one of the first tasks you will be trying in this book is to act like an ape with your partner. Such behavior might seem totally absurd, and in many ways it is (I'll talk more about the importance of absurdity later). But it is also a serious exercise in unencumbered communication.

Just mimicking the slightly hunched, loose-armed posture of a primate immediately changes our frame of reference. It is a softer, relaxed posture, with the emphasis more on brawn than brain. When you add to this the grunts and groans of ape talk, communication becomes truly primitive. There's no way you can act like an ape and use subtle, complicated communication. It is almost impossible to make a power play because of the limited vocabulary imposed. A grunt has only so many variations. It cannot hide feelings; it can only reveal them. There can be an angry grunt, a scared grunt, a demanding grunt, even a questioning grunt. But it's pretty hard to say one thing and mean another when you're going ape. Thus, you send your partner clear signals. There is little room for misinterpretation. Going ape allows you to speak from the heart without feeling as though you are taking such a big risk.

As couples begin to reveal themselves to each other, to be vulnerable and to take risks, they start to feel powerful and strong. They do not give up their identity, feelings, rights, ideas, or actions; an ape is no pushover. Going ape is a refreshing exercise that can, in minutes, breathe life into a stale, troubled relationship. Becoming an ape for a few minutes each day reinforces the fact that you can share feelings with your partner and remain powerful and strong. In fact, you may learn what real power is for the first time in your life.

2. M*e* for I

From apehood, I graduate couples into the "Me Tarzan, you Jane" stage. Words are reintroduced, but in a way that short-circuits the old intellectual patterns. This is done by simply substituting the primitive word *me* for the more heavily charged I. Unfortunately, the overused I sentence has been used typically to control and manipulate one's partner. "I think you should . . . ," "I know you can . . . ," "I think . . . ," and "I feel . . ." all come loaded with accusations, judgments, threats, and power plays. The person who receives these communications feels judged, rejected, or manipulated.

The most insidious of the I sentences is "I feel. . . ." In recent years the words I *feel* have been elevated to a holy status in our society. Psychology books, magazines, and TV talk shows tell us that the highest form of communication is to state our feelings. The problem is that when most of us use the words I *feel*, we are doing just the opposite. We have learned to hide behind this expression. We deceive ourselves into believing we have revealed ourselves and are shocked when we get a hostile response from our partner. We can't understand what went wrong, so we accuse our partner ("You just can't deal with my feelings!"), never imagining that when we said "I feel you don't understand me," we were really saying, "You are selfish and don't give

160

me any attention in this relationship." Our partner responds not to the words but to the underlying message and ends up feeling defensive and hostile because he or she felt accused and misunderstood.

How does substituting *me* for I improve this situation? First of all, the use of *me* introduces an absurdity. Just the fact that the grammar is wrong inhibits the usual dynamic. It immediately signals, "Stop, something different is going on here." The listener is cued not to expect to hear the same old thing, and that interferes with the habitual defensive response.

On a deeper level, the use of the word *me* puts the speaker more directly in touch with himself or herself. To say "I feel sad today" already implies some disconnection from the feelings of sadness: "I" am observing how I feel, and "I" am telling you about my observation. To say "Me sad" is so much more direct. You are no longer watching yourself feel sad; you are in your sadness. You are no longer telling your partner you observe yourself feeling sad; you are showing him or her directly. Better yet, you are revealing your true feelings and are thus giving away a bit of yourself. This sets up a warm, embracing response from your partner, who does not feel controlled or manipulated by your feelings but is able to see them as a simple expression of you.

The use of *me* is also quite childlike. Starting a sentence with the word *me* creates inner associations with the innocence and vulnerability of a child. Try it. It's hard to say, "Me need hug" without feeling quite young and vulnerable. The feeling of vulnerability comes across in your tone, and your partner feels free to respond affectionately. You would probably get the hug. On the other hand, if you were to say, "I want a hug," your request might be received by your partner as a demand, or even a judgment implying, "You never hug me." Your partner would then feel manipulated or threatened and would either hug you grudgingly or give you a lecture on how important it is to learn to fulfill your own needs. Even if you do slip into a judgment ("Me think you should work harder"), your partner will not take seriously what a two-year-old says to him but will hear the real need underneath and answer with reassurance, "Don't worry, me take care of you."

Here's an example of how a couple who had seen me for a while settled an argument by substituting *me* for I. This couple was having a heated battle over his calling her lazy. She became defensive and protested his evaluation of her. In the process of the argument, he realized she was right and he was wrong. (This in itself is pretty amazing, don't you think?) He said, "I'm sorry, but I still don't understand why you reacted so strongly." But the argument didn't end there, because they were still intellectualizing. She answered by explaining, "I'm reacting because you constantly describe me as lazy, and I've been buying it, but now I realize you're wrong. Just look at all I do." She listed her accomplishments. He then cut her off, saying, "Why are you continuing to berate me? I already said I'm sorry." She replied in frustration, "Because you asked me why I got so upset, and I'm telling you." After a brief but tenuous silence, he remembered to use the word *me*. "Me sorry," he said. "Oops, me make mistake." His tonality was childlike and vulnerable. His wife, who was just about ready to launch her backup attack, laughed. She finally felt heard. She forgave him.

She could not forgive him the first time, because though he apologized, he had immediately followed his apology with another accusation (I don't understand why you react so strongly), hidden in the form of a question. When he finally remembered to use the primitive *me*, it gave him the ability to concede without defending his actions. When he did this, she felt satisfied and could accept his apology without having to get in the last word. They both felt safe.

Asking No Questions Asking questions creates big problems in relationships. Questions are a great way to intimidate your partner. When partners ask questions, they believe they are seeking information, but more often than not, they are really involved in accusations, expectations, testing, and guilt slinging. "Where were you last night?" is really a disguised accusation, meaning anything from "I know you were with that woman!" to "So your work is more important than I am." Questions such as "Why do you always push me away?" may not be simple requests for information; in this case the asker might actually be saying, "You're bad for pushing me away."

"Do you love me?"—perhaps the most powerful of all questions—is usually a mechanism for testing your partner. Even a question as innocent as "Did you fill the car with gas?" might really hide an expectation: "I expect you to do these things for me!"

Partners do not react well to questions because on some level they realize there is more here than meets the eye. So questions put them

162

on their guard. They respond to the underlying messages of accusation, expectation, guilt, and testing by using whatever counterintimidation tactic they have developed. In the end, no information at all is shared. The only thing partners get out of this kind of exchange is an argument. The result is more alienation, deprivation, and isolation. Even if one *could* get information by asking a question, it would not be satisfying, because it would not necessarily create intimacy. The results would be the same—alienation, isolation, and deprivation.

Therefore, one of the primary rules of Primitive Communication is to ask no questions. It is amazing how much confusion and suffering can be short-circuited when this simple rule is followed. The wife in one couple who came to see me complained that her husband asked her questions constantly. She felt each question was a setup and that answering it was like walking through a mine field. She never knew when he would blow up at one of her responses. "No matter what I answer, I get nailed," she said. That's because his questions were not requests for information, they were cover-ups for accusations that really masked his need to be noticed. For example, if he asked her, "Did you take out the garbage?" he could mean anything from "I do all the work around here" to "You have no brains" to "How dare you not remember what I tell you to do?" His wife would react to these attacks by withdrawing her love from him.

When I instructed him to give up asking questions, it became clear to both of them how he had used seemingly innocent queries to cover up his own feelings. With the garbage incident, for instance, he was able to state simply his discontent at doing his work as well as hers. Using *me* talk, he stated, "Me do my work only." He was also able to express his need to be noticed by his wife: "Me need you to see how much work me do." Without feeling trapped and accused, his wife felt safe to respond to his real grievances. She became more attentive to remembering to take out the garbage. She also said to him, "You my he-man." He felt appreciated and loved, which is what he really wanted in the first place. She finally felt she was out of the war zone. It was safe to be at home.

It is challenging to stop asking questions. When you try it, you realize how much you depend on them. One couple asked me how to express an invitation without asking a question. The results had profound effects on their relationship. When she had to visit her mother, she would always ask him if he wanted to go. She learned to substitute her feelings and desires in place of a question: "Me need to visit my mother, and me want you to come with me," or "Me need to visit my mother—me go alone today." Her husband knew exactly what she needed from him, did not feel manipulated, and so was free to make a choice.

All of Primitive Communication is based on not asking questions and particularly on not asking "Why?" In traditional therapy, "Why?" is a very important question. But if someone is drowning, you don't ask him why he is in the water; you throw him a lifeline. Primitive Communication is a lifeline. It creates closeness through action, not questions and understanding. As I've stated before, understanding can come later. First come up on deck and know you are really safe and protected.

Touching and Talking Touch is a vital part of any relationship. More than anything else, it can express our tenderness, our warmth, and our nurturance. It offers us much-needed protection and shelter from the struggles of daily life. What would life be without a hug?

But just as high-level verbalization can signal disguised messages to your partner and in return be received in myriad ways, so touch can have the same effect. When this happens, as it does so often, touch becomes one more intimidation tactic. That is why I ask couples to talk when they touch each other.

When you were held as a baby, you were cooed to or sung to or talked to while you were being held, stroked, or tickled. The best contact for you was to be held and to hear such great sounds as "Kootchie, kootchie, koo." If you were held as a child but did not hear sounds, you would feel empty. There would also be a void if you heard sounds and were not held. For some reason, growing up has become synonymous with touching silently—that is, if we were lucky enough to have been touched at all past the age of five. The silent touch is so open to interpretation that it breeds suspicion and we are no longer certain that what we are receiving is really safe. Are you being touched because someone wants something from you ("I need to be taken care of"), to keep you quiet ("Don't yell at me; I didn't mean to lose the keys"), to bribe you ("I'll give you a hug if you wash the dishes"), or to judge you ("My, you're putting on weight")?

Manipulative touching creates confusion and guilt. You feel you should be enjoying the contact—a hug is supposed to make you feel good. So why do you feel like kicking your partner when he puts his arms around you? You begin to imagine there is something wrong with you. It must be that you are just cold and insensitive. Then you feel guilty: "My partner is giving to me. Why am I rejecting him?"

When partners use words while touching each other, the risk of manipulation and misinterpretation is reduced. So on the simplest level, when I ask you to touch your partner's nose and say, "Touch nose," your partner knows that there are no ulterior motives. You are just touching his nose. It is very much the way we behave with children when we are teaching them to recognize their body parts. It is never a dry lesson with a baby. You don't draw a nose on a blackboard and say, "That's your nose." The learning is a warm, loving experience. You touch the baby's nose and say, "Nose," in a soft voice. Then you touch your own nose and say, "Nose." Then maybe the baby touches your nose and says, "Nose." You then applaud the baby's wisdom. He or she giggles in delight. Touching noses becomes the most intimate of experiences when words and touch are used together.

Primitive Communication takes the guesswork out of touching and returns it to the safe, nurturing experience it is meant to be. Saying "Me touch" when you touch your partner indicates you are touching for the pure joy of touching. Saying, "Me take care of you" when you touch indicates you are nurturing your partner. Saying, "Me keep you safe" as you hug your partner means you are offering protection. Messages like these send clear signals to your partner. They are not easily misinterpreted. If you use words when you touch your partner, there can be no mistakes about your intent.

If you have some other message you want to communicate, and particularly if you want something from your partner, don't use touch to get it across. If you want your partner to take care of you, for example, simply say, "Me need care" or even "Me need hug." If you use only touch to communicate this, you will be in trouble. Your partner will feel manipulated, and you will get a hostile response.

One woman I worked with complained that her husband would hug her in the morning when she was busy getting the kids (and herself) ready for the day. She resented what she saw as interference with her morning routine, and as a result she acted brittle and cold. The colder she became, the more her husband criticized her for her lack of warmth. She then accused him of being too needy. She felt resentful and guilty, and he felt deprived and angry.

I instructed the husband to say, "Me need hug" in the morning and then leave the rest up to his wife. This way, he stated his feelings rather than disguising them with touch. Using Primitive Communication, he expressed his need rather than demanding it be met. The demand had brought only rejection, while the direct expression of his need in a vulnerable tone freed his wife to respond by either giving him a hug or not. Though there were times she chose not to, just feeling she had a choice enabled her to respond positively more often. He didn't get hugs all the time, but he got more than before, and the ones he did get felt more satisfying because they were given freely with love. In order to make her feel safe when she hugged her husband, I had her say, "Hug, hug" or "Me give hug." It helped her know she was doing nothing more than giving a hug. Her hug was not a signal that she would have to take care of her husband as well as the kids in the morning. She could give him a quick hug and go on with her business. Knowing that, she actually began to enjoy those few seconds of physical contact.

After I give couples these three tools—primitive language, asking no questions, and touching and talking—many report feeling hopeful about their relationship for the first time in years. This usually occurs in one session, certainly not long enough for me to go into their entire family histories. In one hour they learn how to make each other feel safe, and they experience a big dose of intimacy.

My clients spend an average of only six weeks with me. Even the really "smart" ones, the professionals who are so entrenched in their fancy words and power games, begin to have fun together in just a short time. In this respect, Primitive Communication is as exciting for what it *is not* as for what it is. You don't need all the angst of long-term introspection. In fact, introspection could set you and your partner back, getting you deeper and deeper into the "fear of intimacy" cycle illustrated earlier. Breaking the cycle with Primitive Communication is unbelievably effective—and fast. And a hell of a lot more fun.

Humor and Absurdity The fourth principle of Primitive Communication, the use of humor and absurdity, forms an important element in each of the other tactics; primitive language, asking no questions, and touching and talking would be impossible to implement without humor. Yet in Primitive Communication, humor and absurdity also stand by themselves as a way to achieve intimacy. Intimacy needs a light touch, not a heavy hand. When couples laugh and play together, they feel safe. That's why Primitive Communication is loaded with fun. Even if you are going ape on your own, you can have fun—when your partner expects a harsh response from you, you can surprise him or her with your wit. But only a special kind of humor is appropriate for Primitive Communication. High-level, intellectual humor will not do. It has to be simple, silly, zany, childlike humor. This kind of humor helps couples stop thinking so much. It interferes with the thought patterns that keep the power struggle going and keep partners apart. It is almost impossible to be intimidating when you are using primitive humor. When I ask you to feed your partner applesauce, it is because this kind of silliness stymies the adult cognitive mind. There's nothing to do but have fun.

Today some people are using humor to heal themselves of disease. Norman Cousins, in his now classic book, *Anatomy of an Illness*, tells how he healed himself of a rare disease by belly-laughing at Charlie Chaplin movies for several hours a day. I teach couples to heal their unhealthy relationships in the same way. Silliness can be a powerful medicine.

Along with humor, absurdity plays an important role in fostering intimacy. When you feed your partner, for example, you are doing something completely out of the norm. It is absurd, it is a surprise to your adult rational consciousness. In this way Primitive Communication borrows from Zen Buddhism and other Eastern spiritual disciplines, where the Master bypasses the student's inquiring mind through a sudden or seemingly absurd gesture or question. Unable to deal with it in the usual way, the student is, one hopes, shocked into under- standing that there is a different, more enlightened way to perceive reality than through the limits of intellectual thought.

So it is with Primitive Communication. Through absurdity and humor, I hope to jar you into seeing that what you perceive as reality in your relationship is merely a limited vision. It is amazing how much easier it is to take risks when you bring absurdity into your relation- ship—it breaks down resistance to change. And humor makes accept- ing serendipity and getting intimate painless. There is a kind of magic at work here.

When couples come to me for the first time, they are usually weary from battle. Their faces are serious, and they are poised and ready to defend their positions. Their relationship has either become intolerably intense or has gone dead. After hearing their story, one of the first things I do is introduce some humor. If I can get the couple to laugh with me—or at me—I know I've taken the first step to disrupting their intimidation tactics. To the relationship gone dead, it gives a spark of life; to a relationship plagued by intensity, it brings a moment of relief. Humor has momentarily interrupted the couple's habitual dynamic of relating. In that moment they have the possibility of hearing what I am saying to them. In those brief seconds, a clear space opens in the struggle and pain, and they may be willing to hear what they always believed to be true is not the truth at all. The tasks I assign couples after this initial interaction always involve humor or absurdity. It keeps them off their guard, adds fresh air to the relationship, and fosters trust and safety.

Though I cannot in this book deliver spontaneous humor appropriate to your specific situation, I have tried to convey the same kind of silliness and humor I would if you were in my private office. You will probably think some of the things I have said are outrageous or some of the things I ask you to do are ridiculous. You will be correct in your assumption, but if you don't try my suggestions, you will be missing the point. I *want* you to be silly, zany, childlike, even ridiculous. Your power struggle simply cannot maintain itself in the face of such goings-on.

From Dependencies to Mutual Dependence

Why be in a relationship at all if you cannot depend on each other and trust each other? This is what a relationship is for. This is what intimacy is about. I realize that when many of you see the word *dependence* you might start to think that I don't know what I'm talking about. *Dependence* has become a dirty word in our society. Lately, not needing or depending on anyone else has become a hallmark of health. "Be independent!" is the rallying cry of therapists and one that runs rampant in all the articles we read on how to have a successful relationship. We have all been scared into thinking dependence is some kind of disease. We associate it with weakness, and we try to pretend we don't want it or need it. We believe we can be powerful only if we are independent. I say that the true test of power is our capacity to

168

become mutually dependent on each other, to need and trust another human being.

I am not afraid of the word *dependence*, and I don't want you to be either. It's dependenc*ies* that scare me. Without allowing ourselves to feel dependent and loved and safe, we have no alternative but to fulfill those needs with the kinds of addictive behaviors I described earlier. I do not want couples to be dependent on drugs; I want them to get high on intimacy.

When I tell you to become mutually dependent, I do not mean you should submit or cater to your partner. If you do this, you are placating and colluding, which are tactics of intimidation. I also do not mean you should smother or hang on your partner. These behaviors only reflect distrust and suspicion. When I advocate mutual dependence, I am suggesting that partners allow themselves to need each other and be taken care of by each other. And that they do this with the full trust that they will not be consumed, submerged, or taken over by the other. Mutual dependence means nurturing each other and not dominating each other. When we keep ourselves detached and separate, it is a form of domination. Of course, each partner in a couple needs time alone. But when time alone is the only thing the person can tolerate, something is very wrong.

Some people might say to themselves, "What if my partner dies or leaves and I find myself alone?" or "If I have become dependent on my partner, I will not know how to live by myself." If a time comes when you must be alone, you will deal with it then. Why deprive yourself of the joy of letting your partner nurture you when he or she is here for that now? It's stupid to act as if you are alone when you have the possibility for so much joy and fun. If you do ever face life alone, you will feel important, worthwhile, and lovable to the extent you allowed your partner to care for you. You will then be good company for yourself.

The act of sharing your life in a close relationship with your partner is an act of living at its best. All the theory in the world will not give you this experience. Going ape will.

BACK TO THE BASICS

Oops! If you read the preceding section, and this remedial insight caused you to think too much, you may now be in a state of tension. I can't leave you with all of that stress and high-level thought process. I have got to get you back to the basics. I have to unclutter your mind in order to prepare you again for low-level risk taking, for Primitive Communication.

Now, no more of this remedial insight. Let's get back to the basics, back to monkey business. Get your favorite crayon and color your partner's ear:

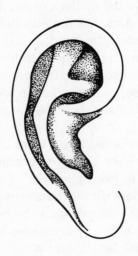

Then look at the picture and say, "Ear."
Go to the next page.

With your crayon, color your partner's nose:

Then look at the picture and say, "Nose."
Go to the next page.

With your crayon, color your partner's chin:

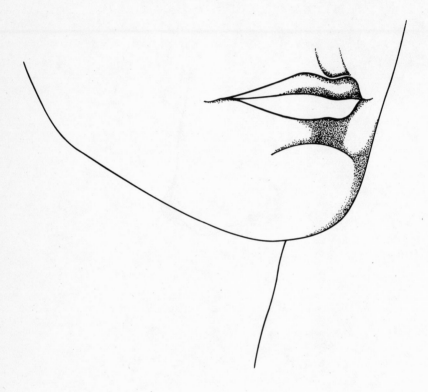

Then look at the picture and say, "Chin."
Go to the next page.

With your crayon, color your partner's lips:

Then look at the picture and say, "Lips."
Go to the next page.

Show your partner the pictures you just colored. Touch your partner's lips and say, "Lips." Smile at your partner. Again, touch your partner's lips and say, "Me kiss." Kiss your partner, but remember to smack your lips and make plenty of noise.

I hope you feel good, because I feel much better. I can now leave you without worrying about the effect of remedial insight.

Me happy we shared this experience. Me wish you well on your journey toward intimacy. Bye-bye.

Some Questions and Answers About Primitive Communication

Q. *Is Primitive Communication a formula for instant intimacy?*
A. I have met so many couples who want their intimacy placed in a microwave oven. I wish we could program intimacy in seconds, but this is not the case. It is a slow, evolving process; the tactics may be quick, but the feelings take time to develop. It takes time to build confidence and trust. It takes time because you may have talked for years about intimacy, but you may have avoided it for decades. I am interested in direction. If you proceed in the right direction, then you can build on victories.

We always seem to be searching for excuses for why we cannot be close to a partner: "He rejected me last time I wanted sex." "She was rude to my mother." The experience of closeness creates an amnesia about all of the old hurts, those historical events that you remember and focus on. These events and stories become weak as you stop using questions, touch and talk, and use primitive language. As intimidation and intensity are reduced in a relationship, then warmth and humor grow. As we think less and experience more, we feel less alone and we can again begin to trust. As we become more vulnerable, our emotional scars begin to disappear.

Q. *Can passion return to a relationship?*
A. Yes, passion can return. If you have almost talked your relationship to death, then the return of passion will depend upon your use of Primitive Communication. The experience of passion involves the nonthinking, risk-taking part of you. Some partners think that passion can be maintained through sexuality. Passion can still be extinguished even though sexuality is being maintained. This is because passion depends more on your courage to be open than on being sexual. The best idea is to be open emotionally—then passion can be displayed in many areas, including the sexual arena. To get to this openness, you must give up control, in which, through intimidating behavior, passion becomes slowly extinguished. Control blocks passion.

Give up control and use primitive language and behaviors. You may then put out the welcome sign—Welcome Home, Passion.

Q. *Does everything have to be spelled out, or can I make certain assumptions?*
A. Assumptions will not work.

Assume nothing and repeat basic feelings of caring for the rest of your life.

If you assume that your partner knows that you care, then you are taking a major risk. Your partner may not know, but even if he or she does know, you still must let him or her know that you care. If your partner suffers from feelings of abandonment or fears being controlled, then your intimate language suppresses these fears. Tell your partner about your feelings of love, but do it sincerely. Too many couples use "love" and professions of love as an intimidation tactic. A nice "Me love you" and a noisy kiss will do.

Q. *If my partner becomes intimate, will I go into intimacy shock?*
A. Yes, you could go into intimacy shock. You'll feel this shock if you become distrustful about things getting better too quickly. You might do several things. You may withdraw, attack, become angry or depressed, even become overjoyed. After years of deprivation, intimacy may be a shock to your system.

Do not worry if you go into intimacy shock. It will be short-lived. As you give up loneliness and suffering, you both begin to build up your acceptance of pleasure. I do know that if you and your partner have made a long-term commitment to loneliness and suffering, you need to be eased gently into the world of warmth and affection.

If you feel that the intimacy shock is too severe, then ask your partner for smaller daily doses. I do not want you to overdose on intimacy and then yearn for a rapid return to intimidation. For you, I do recommend a slow decompression process. Your capacity for intimacy will slowly build up, and you'll find that you need more warmth and affection.

Q. *Will Primitive Communication prevent divorce?*
A. Primitive Communication may not prevent a divorce, nor should it prevent divorces in some cases. But it will help partners see the real reasons for the divorce. So many couples get divorced because they find fault with each other's drug use, infidelity, gambling, anger, abuse, or inability to manage finances, but the underlying power struggle is not dealt with. This power struggle may continue even after a couple is divorced, because they never learned the language of intimacy. After a divorce, many partners continue the struggle through their children. The pain never seems to end.

If we could only talk in an open and nurturing way to our partner, much of this craziness would not have to dominate our lives. When you have intimate communication, if one partner does get into trouble, at least the other has a chance at dealing with the specific problem rather than allowing the power struggle to build into crisis proportions. The crisis will stimulate more crises, and eventually judgmentalism will overpower the relationship and it will crack. Even after a relationship folds, if the communication problem is not dealt with, you will continue to be involved in some difficult power struggle with your next partner. The changing of a partner will initially bring relief from the struggle, but this honeymoon is short-lived. So before changing partners, change your language and go ape.

Q. *What if I did not choose the right partner?*
A. "Did I choose the right partner?" That pops up even in the best of relationships. I do not want you to get too much mileage out of this question, because the answer is simple. Yes, yes, yes. There is a better partner out there for you; there is also a worse partner out there for you.

I prefer to look at this question from a different viewpoint. I prefer

177

the question "Can I grow with my partner?" If both partners are open to change and growth, then both can also learn intimate behavior. This openness to growth is more important than the idea of whether someone is right for you. Even if two people are right for each other, the relationship can get into deep trouble if the openness necessary for growth is not there.

The question of someone being right for you is instilled in us through the culture of romance. When children read love stories, everyone lives happily ever after. As children, we are seduced by romance into looking for the right person. I wish this romantic literature would seduce us into looking for someone we could grow with. This growth seeking would help us mature, while seeking Mr./Ms. Right causes us to be narrow when looking for an available partner.

Once you learn how to grow together, a strong bond of friendship develops and the person you choose becomes the right one.

Q. *How can I use Primitive Communication to get what I need from my partner?*
A. All of life involves bargaining, compromising, and making concessions. A successful relationship depends on your ability to bargain successfully. After all, you are two different people with different needs and thoughts and desires. You may even come from different cultures or ethnic backgrounds. From something as simple as deciding which movie to see to something as emotionally charged as whether or not to make love, in a relationship there are always two people's needs to deal with. It is natural to be different. What is unnatural is to let those differences drive you apart.

The problem is most people have never learned the art of bargaining. Instead, they act out various tactics designed to get them their way through intimidation. These tactics run the gamut from screaming, threatening, judging, and cajoling to the silent treatment, getting sick, whining, and conceding grudgingly.

With PC, bargaining is clear and simple. Partners state their desires in clear, obvious language: "Me need hug." "Me go movies tonight." "Me need to make love." With statements like these you reveal your position, you signal what you are willing to do, and you also signal what your limits are. With this information your partner can begin negotiations in a healthy, honest way. You have not intimidated, judged, coerced, or inflicted your opinions on your partner, so he is free to respond according to real needs. "No, me no feel like making love tonight, but me give foot massage instead."

Perhaps you didn't get your exact needs met at this time, but you did get a concession that felt warm and good. This is what bargaining is all about. Had you asked, "Do you want to make love tonight?" instead of using a *me* statement, your question would have revealed nothing about your needs and you probably would have received a flat "no" in response. This might have then led to an argument over your not getting enough sex. A far cry from lying close together in bed, having your toes rubbed. When you know how to bargain correctly, you will be able to make concessions like these, which will satisfy both of you.

Q. *Do I have the right to say no to my partner?*
A. Of course you can say no. The problem occurs in how you say no. You do not have the right to make judgments and set expectations that manipulate your partner, making him or her feel guilty or forcing him or her to submit to your needs. That only leads to more warfare. You need to say no in a way that reveals you as a person and not you as a controlling individual.

You do not have a right to say, "I won't go on your company's picnic, because I find your clients offensive." This is an attack on your partner's work. Just reveal your level of discomfort and say, "Me feel uncomfortable going to your company's picnic." This is not an attack. This could lead to a discussion of your feelings, which are important for your partner to hear. However, even after this discussion, either your "no" stands or you may want to renegotiate, but the point is that you still have the right to say no.

Q. *What should I do with my anger toward my partner?*
A. You can hold on to anger for an hour, day, week, month, or year. But at some point you must let your partner know what you are feeling. If you express your feelings in hostile and judgmental ways, your partner will become defensive and the anger will keep recycling itself. You both get into a spiral of expressing anger, and it keeps going. It takes on a life of its own, and your lives end up spent in anger. I have met too many partners who pay homage to anger. Laughter and intimacy almost never enter their relationship.

When I speak to couples about how they use anger in their relationship, I usually hear the statement "It just happens—I get angry, and I can't control it." You may believe this, but I do not. You are far from helpless when you act out your anger. Whether you express your anger by screaming, withdrawing, hitting, or fainting, you are engaged in punitive tactics that only endanger your relationship. If you are angry, then express it in a nonpunitive way. Say, "Me angry." You will be heard, and you will not be avoiding intimacy.

With Primitive Communication you bypass this cycle of intimacy avoidance. Once you express your feelings in nonjudgmental ways, your partner can more easily understand your grievances and respond appropriately.

Q. *Can I manipulate my partner using Primitive Communication?*
A. Yes, you can be manipulative using Primitive Communication. I call this effective manipulation if it leads to intimacy. So keep manipulating your partner with Primitive Communication. One day you may want to reveal this manipulation to your partner by saying, "You know, I have been manipulating you with Primitive Communication. All of that love stuff and affection we have been experiencing is because I have been careful not to judge you, and I have been nurturing you by revealing my feelings using primitive sentences and words."

Your partner will say, "Yes, that's great; keep it up."

Q. *Can Primitive Communication be used destructively?*
A. Almost anything can be used destructively, so why not Primitive Communication? If you say to your partner, "Me abuse you," this would be a destructive application of Primitive Communication. I doubt, however, that you have used words of affection to strike out at your partner. I also doubt that you would try to to hurt your relationship with the tactics I have recommended.

If you want to hurt your partner, I am sure that you have developed an arsenal of intimidation tactics over the years. I also know that you do not have to add Primitive Communication to this arsenal.

Q. *After we learn Primitive Communication, will we have a relapse?*
A. Yes, there will be relapses. You may occasionally slip back to your old ways, but with continued practice of Primitive Communication your relapses will be shorter and less frequent.

Once you have experienced intimacy by using Primitive Communication, you and your partner will find it more difficult to intimidate each other. When you go back to your old behavior, you will both miss the fun of being close to one another.

If you are in a relapse, don't worry. Trust that your skills will return. To ensure their quick return, just go back to the basic warm-up at the beginning of this book.

Q. *Do I have to use Primitive Communication forever?*
A. No, you just have to experience intimacy forever. Once you become intimate, then any language can be used. You may want to experiment with French, sign language, drum beats, Morse code, or even some type of primitive computer. Once you know how to be intimate, you can let your creativity fly. Primitive Communication stimulates intimacy, and I am sure that you will be creative in ways of continuing this stimulation.

Q. *Do men and women bring different fears to a relationship?*
A. I often see a different fear pattern in men than I do in women. Men are frequently fearful of being controlled, and women are frequently fearful of being abandoned. Both sexes have these fears, but I do sense this differential pattern.

There are many reasons why this pattern could exist, all of which are open to multiple interpretations. If men are taught culturally to be dominant, if their fathers tried to establish control, or if their mothers dominated their fathers, we have the beginnings of these fears for men. For women, it is easy to speculate that they saw their mother trying to control the household while their father withdrew or ran from the relationship. All of these speculations have found their way into the psychological literature. These fears could be transmitted to partners through all sorts of mechanisms. Typically, if a man is prematurely sexual toward a woman, he is seen as trying to use sex to establish control. If a woman wants a premature commitment from a man, she is seen as trying to prevent abandonment.

These fears can be exposed in the ways partners talk to each other. If you fear abandonment, you may keep asking your partner, "Where have you been?" or "Why didn't you call?" If you fear being controlled, you may tell your partner, "Don't tell me what to do," or "I don't have to account to you for every second of my day."

I ask partners to use Primitive Communication to deal with these fears. If a partner fears abandonment, I have her say to her partner, "Me need to be with you." I ask her partner to respond with "Me protect you." This calms the abandonment fear. She feels less of a need to control him in hidden ways. It also calms his fear of being controlled, because she is direct with her feelings.

If a partner fears being controlled, I will tell him to say, "Me do for me," and the partner to say, "Me hear you." This calms the control fear. He has now set boundaries for himself. I predict that his partner will cooperate with his boundaries because his clarity reduces her fear of abandonment.

Let's look at an example.

One husband I worked with came home every night, put on the TV, and dedicated his evening to football. His wife wanted him to talk to her. He saw her demand as nagging and scolding. She felt his attachment to the TV as abandonment. The more she nagged, the more silent he became. No one was satisfied. I asked him to respond to her needs by saying, "Me tackle you after game." This helped him set a boundary and take control in a way that assuaged her fears of abandonment. I had her say, "We score points after game." By saying this, she agreed not to nag him during the game. He felt less controlled, which made him more amenable to meeting her needs later. After the game they spoke and had some time for closeness. The other way they just engaged in warfare.

Q. *But my girlfriend/boyfriend wants something more from me—and we've been dating only six weeks.*

A. The problem of female anxiety over abandonment and male anxiety over control leads to certain behaviors during courtship. A man may try to become overly sexual without having established a real relationship with his new date. This gives him a false sense of security, because if she submits sexually, then he has less anxiety over the control issue. Meanwhile, women may act out their fear of abandonment with a premature commitment demand. A woman may try to extract a commitment without really having a relationship with her date. This power struggle leads to all sorts of incorrect interpretations, and neither party feels safe.

When a man tells me that a woman is resisting sexual advances, I try to explain to him that she may not be ready at that moment, but that she may be ready after several dates. He may resist this time sequence and say, "I'm ready now, and I am not ready to make a commitment for tomorrow." I then point out that he is resisting sexuality over a period of time and is really using sex as a way of hiding his fear of being controlled. At the same time, if a female is complaining to me that her date is too aggressive, I will point out that he is hiding his fear of being controlled and that she should not interpret his desire for early sexual contact as a rejection of her as an individual or as a sign of commitment. I also point out that if she demands premature commitment, she may not trust that he is really there for her. She may say that she does not want casual sex. I reply, "Neither would you want a casual marriage."

I try to tell females that male sexual overtures need to be decoded beyond the physical advance offering. If she retracts because he "wants one thing," then she may not be decoding his fear of control. So rather than suppressing the offering with the typical statement "I don't want casual sex," it might be preferable to say (if she is attracted to him), "I am so flattered by *your* honesty that even though I am not ready to be physical, I do want you to know that I will be completely honest with you." This alleviates his fear of being controlled and his need to use sex as a power/submission tactic.

I try to tell men that women are not being controlling if they do not submit initially to sexual advances. The denial of sexuality should not be interpreted as a control mechanism. I explain that she fears if she gets close he may abandon her. So when he states, "Why couldn't she just respond to the moment? Is she frigid?" I explain, "After the act, she wants to have more contact. Are you also available next weekend?" The typical male reply will be "How do I know what I want to do next weekend?" I then reveal a paradox by pointing out that he is avoiding sexual contact for the next weekend and is not as sexual as he states. I also point out that this attitude could be interpreted by the female as a preabandonment statement. Perhaps it would be better to say, "I would love to be sexual today, but I'm going to put that feeling on hold and ask for us to see each other next weekend so we can become better acquainted." This reduces her experience of premature abandonment, and he feels more in control and does not suffer premature control feelings.

183

Q. How did you get started using Primitive Communication?
A. I was trained in traditional Western psychology. This traditional method involves understanding why a partnership is in trouble and, from this understanding, finding different ways of getting close. This understanding approach is based on rational thinking and understanding facts.

With this method I found that while some couples were helped, many others were harmed. I also found that in training graduate students to engage in rational forms of intervention, they would become inflexible and serve as models of inflexibility. I began to search for other models, and I came under the influence of Eastern philosophy, which deals with a nonrational path. It focuses on acting and experiencing feelings rather than just talking about feelings.

A wonderful example is if you were to go to a Zen master and ask to be taught experience. You might be whacked over the head. The Zen master would give you the experience of feeling and not help you think about the experience. This nonthinking or spiritual path influenced my way of training graduate students and how I work with couples. This method freed me to begin to experiment with various types of communication techniques, which led me to the development of Primitive Communication.

With an Eastern philosophical approach, couples are taught to think less and experience more, which leads them to become less judgmental of each other. To think less frees you from judgments. This is a paradox because the commonly accepted idea is that couples get into trouble because they do not think enough. The reality of the situation is that couples need to think less and do more.

To get couples to do more, whacking is needed. Just as the Zen master "whacks" the seeker of experience, the topics and tactics in this book are intended to "whack" the reader into beginning to experience. An exercise I ask you to do may appear to be silly, but the meaning behind it is important to the relationship. It may involve trust, sharing, caring, and giving. Now, if I told you all that, the exercise would be too "important" to you. You'd think too much. You might even be afraid you would get it wrong. The tactics were written so as to encourage you to take a risk and not to immobilize yourself with thought.

So this is really how I got started, by whacking. But submitting yourself to whacking takes great courage. It takes courage to simplify one's life, while it takes little courage to make our lives complex. We hide behind complexity and then use the excuse that we do not have enough time or energy. We can hide behind material goods, clothing, makeup, degrees, and complex language to disguise our needs. When we really strip ourselves and face ourselves in an honest and open way, we do not like to be alone; we need to care for others and let others care for us.

To get partners to engage in this simplification process, I also had to simplify my approach. After all, how can I preach simplification and risk taking while at the same time keep my therapeutic approach at a complex level? I had to be a model; I had to strip myself of my complex theoretical Western approach and model the Eastern approach. This was the start of Primitive Communication.

Q. Is *Primitive Communication just a gimmick*?
A. No, PC is not a gimmick. It is a tool. A tool that will make the work of becoming intimate easier.

Q. Can *Primitive Communication be used outside a relationship*?
A. Perhaps the future will have surprises for all of us in the area of language skills and intimacy. Just as we study foreign languages, we may eventually study the language of intimacy. In the future, I can see the use of audio tapes and videotapes as a way of learning intimacy. I can see precommitment meetings between couples and an intimacy language specialist; this specialist could also be used for preseparation and predivorce meetings.

Education may one day focus on intimacy and language. Today we can walk into a school, attend a coed class on sexuality, and view this as a normal part of the school day. One day we may walk into the same school and see students learning about intimacy. After all, if we teach about sexuality, shouldn't we also teach about getting close to another human being?

Do not go bananas if you are a member of the English Department. I am not recommending that your students substitute Me for I, but I do feel that students need to learn more about language, behavior, and attitudes. I also have said that I hope Mom and Dad will not substitute Me for I in front of Junior, because Junior will get poor grades in grammar. And obviously, your colleagues at work will question your sanity if you do it with them. You may, however, want to try it with your parents, as discussed earlier in the book.

Q. *It sounds like, besides helping couples, Primitive Communication can also be a philosophy of living.*
A. Yes, Primitive Communication goes beyond the words couples use with each other. Primitive Communication also involves a philosophy of living. It emphasizes simplicity and low technology. I am not antitechnology, but I am prorelationships. Our involvement with technologies has made us focus on going to Mars rather than looking at ourselves. If we begin to make our lives less complex, we also make ourselves less complex, and this process is needed to strengthen relationships. Material acquisition has become associated with power, but real power is learning to be open and mutually interdependent. I find that people do not know what their real power is.

The media add to this confusion when they associate power with specific symbols such as high-powered automobiles or the false power of a person on a horse smoking a select brand of cigarettes. Primitive Communication teases us into seeing our incorrect assumptions and teaches us how to get on the path to real power. To hug and cry, to show in a direct and simple way who we are, is the power in all of us.

Q. *Julie, do you use Primitive Communication?*
A. Yes, me do. Me now say bye-bye.

Appendix A: Reminder Card

Photocopy this reminder card. Place this card in your wallet next to your organ donation card.

REMINDER CARD

1. Ask no questions.
2. Touch and talk.
3. Use *Me* for *I*.
4. Be absurd

Appendix B: Primitive Calling Card

Many people seem to derive status from calling cards. Here is a sample primitive calling card that will probably help to lower your status in society:

Me named _____

Me dwell at _____

Me can be phoned at _____

*Gender   "Me have a Pipi"

                  "Me have a Petunia"

*Identify your gender by choosing one statement. Omit the other. If you are confused, then leave both statements on your card.

Appendix C: Primitive Bookmark

Photocopy this primitive bookmark. Give it as a gift to your partner.

Me Nuts About
this Page
and
Me Nuts About
YOU

Appendix D: Inspirational Sayings

Sometimes it helps to be inspired by a saying. You may want to photocopy a saying, frame it, and place it above your bed. Here is a sampling of some great quotes that have inspired me.

The greatest sin of our age is to make the concrete abstract.

Nicholas Berdyaev

The language of friendship is not words, but meanings.

Henry Thoreau

Logic is like the sword—those who appeal to it shall perish by it.

Samuel Butler

Fortunately psycho-analysis is not the only way to resolve inner conflicts. Life itself still remains a very effective therapist.

Karen Horney

It's not the men in my life that count; it's the life in my men.

Mae West

To appreciate nonsense requires a serious interest in life.

Gelett Burgess

The man who listens to reason is lost; reason enslaves all whose minds are not strong enough to master her.

George Bernard Shaw

We put people in the hospital because they have delusions. If I have a delusion, they call it a theory.

Carl Whitaker

The serenity of a nap can only be equaled by the potency of one banana.

Julius Rosen

Sources

Bernstein, B. "Social class, speech systems, and psycho-therapy. *The British Journal of Sociology*, Vol. 15, March 1964.

Cousins, N. *Anatomy of an Illness as Perceived by the Patient: Reflections on Healing and Regeneration*. New York: Norton & Co., 1979.

Turner and Gross. "An Approach to Family Therapy: an Effective Rule-altering Model." *Journal of Family Counseling*, Vol. 4, No. 1, 1976.

Watts, A. W. *Does It Matter? Essays on Man's Relation to Materiality*. New York: Pantheon Books, 1968.

Watts, A. W. *In My Own Way. An Autobiography*, 1915–1965. Pantheon Books, 1972.

Watts, A. W. *The Spirit of Zen: A Way of Life, Work, and Art in the Far East*. New York: Grove Press, 1958.

Watts, A. W. *The Way of Zen*. New York: Pantheon Books, 1957.

Watzlawick, P. *How Real Is Real?* New York: Random House, 1976.

Watzlawick, P., Weakland, J. H., and Fisch, R. *Change: Principles of Problem Formation and Problem Resolution*. New York: W. W. Norton, 1974.

Whitaker, C. In J. R. Neil and D. P. Kniskern, eds. *From Psyche to System: The Evolving Therapy of Carl Whitaker*. New York: Guilford, 1982.